CW00731777

Blake and Antiquity

Kathleen
Raine

Blake and Antiquity

With a new introduction by the author

 London and New York

First published in the United Kingdom 1979
by Routledge & Kegan Paul

First published in Routledge Classics 2002
by Routledge
2 Park Square, Milton Park, Abingdon, Oxon OX14 4RN
711 Third Avenue, New York NY 10017

Routledge is an imprint of the Taylor & Francis Group

Blake and Antiquity is an abridged version of *Blake and Tradition*,
The A. W. Mellon Lectures in the Fine Arts, 1962 The National
Gallery of Art, Washington D.C.

© 1963, 1968, 1977 Trustees of the National Gallery of Art,
Washington D.C.

Introduction to the Routledge Classics edition © 2002 Kathleen Raine

Typeset in Joanna by RefineCatch Limited, Bungay, Suffolk

British Library Cataloguing in Publication Data
A catalogue record for this book is available from the British Library

ISBN 978-0-415-28581-0 (hbk)
ISBN 978-0-415-28582-7 (pbk)

CONTENTS

INTRODUCTION TO THE
ROUTLEDGE CLASSICS EDITION

Among the wonders of my childhood (I was born in 1908) were little packets from far-away Japan of dyed and dried fragments of pith that, when you put them in a bowl of water, expanded into a water-garden of coloured flowers. Or, to pursue the same thought, every acorn contains a minute oak, every horse-chestnut a potential chestnut tree. To take the idea into the microscopic world, a DNA potential can become a unique human being in all our complexity. Yet an acorn is not an oak-tree, nor a DNA potential a human being. The seminal is the mystery of life, of bird and beast, forest and weed, unknown to the 'virtual reality' of *techne*. So it is with ideas – at some historical moments humankind has been concerned with seminal myths, at others the unfolding of these myths in what C.G. Jung has called 'individuation'. The seminal myth, for example, of Eros can be found in Blake's eight-line poem *The Sick Rose*, in the fairy-tale of Beauty and the Beast, in Canova's beautiful sculpture of Cupid and Psyche, or in every girl's first love. Or all these levels may be found together, from the metaphysical to the psychological and the individual, in a full experience of erotic love, with its ambiguous identity of the 'invisible worm', the serpent, the 'beast' and the divinely beautiful god, Psyche's invisible lover. What lies at the heart of life remains, as it must, a mystery, unknowable.

Re-reading in 2001 this shortened version of *Blake and Tradition* (1963, published in 1977), it seems to me comparable to those Japanese water-flowers, or the acorn that is the potential oak-tree, to which it bears little resemblance. Easier to understand now, I believe, for the intervening years of the twentieth century have seen the advent of the science (or art) of psychology, opened first by Freud and later transformed and enriched by Jung, without whose terms it would be hard to understand the order of reality Blake was expressing in his mythology of 'the Giant Albion', the English nation. All the sacred scriptures of the world are now available in paperback, which at the time my book was written were studied only by scholars or esoteric societies. Now they have become the 'holy books' of a whole generation 'in search of a soul' as Jung has put it, of whom Blake himself is the 'Master'. Growing numbers, and not only of a younger generation, are discovering that the atheist materialism, which remains the orthodoxy of the press, the media and indeed the universities of the modern West, is not only intolerable, but groundless.

In order to make sense of this short book the reader would, it seems to me, to have had to read the two-volume work, *Blake and Tradition*, from which it has been abridged, and to understand that book would have had to spend many years, as I did, immersed in the mythologies, the sacred texts, and the innumerable stories of the world which ultimately are, as the Veda says, but one story, 'written by God'.

Of the mythology of the Giant Albion, the English nation, and of the conflicts and reconciliation of the 'four Zoas' we are ourselves the enactors. They four are in us all, and, once recognised, strangely familiar: Urizen, blind and aged, the tyrant Reason who lays claim to the authority which belongs to the 'Divine Humanity', 'Jesus the Imagination', the God within. Urizen is the gloomy law-giver who declared 'Now I am god from eternity to eternity', framer of the Ten Commandments. Orc is the fiery spirit of energy, the youthful revolutionary, who is Eros, of whom Blake writes 'When Thought is clos'd in Caves, Then love shall show its root in deepest Hell'; *tamasic* Tharmas; and Los, spirit of inspiration, who labours at his 'furnaces', with his hammer creating and destroying the works of Time in his task which is to embody on earth the vision of eternity. It is Los of whom Blake wrote that 'He kept the Divine Vision in time of trouble'. All these are to be found in the great works and in the great shortcomings of English thought throughout history.

It is not difficult to give names to persons who have embodied these archetypes: Urizen in Blake's threefold enemy of the Imagination, Bacon, Newton and Locke; Los, the visionary, is Milton, 'the inspired man', to whom Blake dedicated his 'prophetic' book *Milton*. Blake saw that drama not as a story of 'sin' and 'repentance' as taught by the churches, but, as for Plotinus and the Neoplatonists, of 'sleep' and 'awaking'. Albion is 'sunk in deadly sleep', and throughout his prophetic writings Blake summons the nation to 'awake'. Plotinus, whose works Blake knew in the translations of his one-time friend Thomas Taylor, describes humankind as passing 'from bed to bed, from sleep to sleep'. Blake wrote 'I do not consider either the just or the wicked to be in a Supreme State, but to be every one of them States of Sleep which the soul may fall into in its deadly dreams of Good & Evil when it leaves Paradise following the Serpent.' For Blake the arts are the agents of that awakening, and represent the awakened state: 'Poetry, Painting & Music, the three Powers in Man of conversing with Paradise, which the Flood' – the 'sea of time and space' – 'did not Sweep away.' Therefore, Blake's

Milton, the poet, is called 'the awakener'. The spiritually unawakened are that 'slumbrous mass' who

> Charge visionaries with deceiving
> Or call Men wise for not Believing

It is these who speak of 'the real world' as the world perceived in the unawakened state, but it is only in the awakened state that we see reality as it is. Since the 'Divine Humanity', Blake's 'Jesus, the Imagination', is the 'God within', present in and to every individual, we can always discover that Presence, that source, in ourselves. So understood, Blake's message 'To the Christians', is for us all:

> I give you the end of a golden string
> Only wind it into a ball,
> It will bring you in at Heaven's gate
> Built in Jerusalem's wall.

Christianity, we must remember, is for Blake the religion of 'Jesus, the Imagination', for the whole of humankind. It is for us to 'individuate' the universal life.

I can only hope that my writings on Blake have put into the hands of some seekers for that reality within, the end of Blake's Golden String. They will find, as I have done, that this string is a very long one, winding in not only Blake's own voluminous writings but all the 'sacred' literature of the world, all poetry, music and painting that speaks from and to the Imagination in the forgotten but universal language of Paradise.

The second chapter of *Jerusalem* is dedicated 'To the Jews' and is prefaced by the words

> Ye are united, O ye Inhabitants of Earth, in One Religion, The Religion of Jesus, the most Ancient, the Eternal & the Everlasting Gospel.

This religion is not the Christian Church, but the 'perennial philosophy', the *sanatana dharma* of the Indian mainstream, and in this context, the Jewish tradition of Adam Kadmon. Having named 'Abraham, Heber, Shem and Noah, who were Druids', Blake continues:

> You have a tradition, that Man anciently contain'd in his mighty limbs all things in Heaven & Earth: this you received from the Druids. But now the Starry Heavens are fled from the mighty limbs of Albion.

Adam Kadmon is the human race as a whole, the one-in-many and many-in-one who is the source of Blake's own 'divine humanity', 'as One Man all the Universal family'. Blake has but renamed the Jewish Adam Kadmon, 'Jesus, the Imagination'. We ourselves are that 'universal family' of whom Blake wrote that 'contracting their Exalted Senses, / They behold Multitude, or Expanding they behold as one'. 'Contracting' we individuate, 'Expanding' we participate in the universal vision. In these realities of the Imagination it is, under whatever name, for all to participate.

London, February 2002

Introduction to the First Edition

The text of this book, given as the A. W. Mellon Lectures in the Fine Arts at the National Gallery of Art, Washington, D.C., in 1962, is an abridgment from a longer work, *Blake and Tradition* (Bollingen Series XXXV: 11, 2 vols.). Nothing in the text has been altered, and the plates are taken from *Blake and Tradition*.

These lectures contain the essential theme of the larger book—a thesis more acceptable in 1977 than fifteen years ago, when I sought to establish, in detail which may now seem overelaborate, Blake's indebtedness to Neo-Platonic and other sources within what may be called the canon of the Western esoteric tradition.

With few exceptions, earlier attempts to understand Blake had discounted this tradition—not unnaturally, since it comprises what may be called the excluded knowledge of the current contemporary scientific humanism. The best scholarship had at that time been devoted to the historical and social background of Blake's work and thought, and to his visual sources. But the view was too long current that Blake's ideas, symbols, and mythology were of his own invention; he was the great "original," the uneducated visionary who owed nothing to tradition. This in practice very often meant that the interpretation of his symbolic themes was a guessing game, or a projection of some favorite system (Freudian, Jungian, Marxist, or purely personal) upon his writings. At bottom the difficulty lay in the impossibility of making sense of Blake in terms of current presuppositions. Naturally, critics tried to fit his work into existing critical categories, applicable enough to writers who shared, more or less, the same cultural tradition as themselves. Because he did not do so, it was tempting to assume that Blake was outside tradition altogether.

I began my own studies by attempting to read every work and every author referred to by Blake. Having done so (more or less) I discovered, as others who have done the same (and I think especially of George Mills Harper, whose findings coincided with mine in so many respects, although at that time we had worked independently), that Blake was drawing upon a tradition rich in literature, age-old, continuous, coherent, whose members were as reputable as Plato and Plotinus. This great body of excluded knowledge has long been unacceptable, not on account of its inaccessibility, still less its paucity, but because its premises run counter to those of a materialist civilization.

But Blake was the prophet of a "New Age," a new age now upon us as the "Age of Aquarius" in its anti-materialist birth-throes. And a new age, if it means anything, means a change of premises, of the first principles upon which a civilization is built. Blake's greatest disciple and the first commentator upon his esoteric "system," W. B. Yeats, announcing the end of a cycle and the advent of the "rough beast," was but following Blake. "The rise of soul against intellect, now beginning in the world," announced by Yeats, has brought with it a return to the excluded knowledge—Neo-Platonism, alchemy, astrology, Cabbala—besides the more recent studies of Indian metaphysics, comparative mythology, psychical research, and the psychology of the unconscious. All these and other related fields of knowledge, once dismissed piecemeal, are now seen to belong to a coherent way of understanding and exploring what we choose to call "reality." Blake was familiar with most of the literature available in English—the only language he knew well—relating to the esoteric tradition.

It is difficult to understand why, unless because his doctrine was deeply unwelcome, the name of Thomas Taylor the Platonist, "the English pagan," was not earlier associated with that of Blake. The first translator of Plato and Plotinus into English was certainly a central figure in the Romantic revival. Besides Blake, Taylor's sphere of influence drew in Coleridge, Shelley, Samuel Palmer, perhaps even Keats. When these lectures were first published many Blake scholars were still determined to not know about Taylor; but times have changed. What I then labored to establish by accumulated detail is now increasingly taken for granted. Nor is it any longer possible to dismiss Thomas Taylor from the scene; it is now known that Blake and Taylor were on intimate terms, at least for a time. Scholarship has come to the aid of common sense, and James King has given us, from the Meredith papers, a lifelike picture of the two sages: the Platonist, characteristically demonstrating to Blake step by step some Euclidian theorem, and our visionary exclaiming, "Ah, never mind that—what's the use of going to prove it. Why, I see with my eyes that it is so, and do not require any proof to make it clearer."

I am only too happy that so much that at the time of writing seemed suspect or incredible now seems, on the contrary, axiomatic. I hope nevertheless that some of the "minute particulars" which gave me such delight in the discovery will communicate something of the same delight to a younger generation of Blake lovers. Of course the details given in such a book as this from the wealth of source-material are only the tip of a submerged continent of knowledge—a country with which Blake was familiar—and I can only report, from my own explorations, that this Lost Atlantis is a land of treasures and marvels. Blake's "golden string" leads not only through his own labyrinth, but is the clue leading to so much more. Neo-Platonism, with its mythology and symbolism, is indeed the local European idiom (as Coomaraswamy would say) of a universal and unanimous tradition. Those sources from which Blake drew his knowledge —and in our own century, Jung, Yeats, and increasing numbers of their followers—are learning of the imagination itself. The excluded knowledge of the last two or three centuries seems likely to become the sacred scriptures of a New Age for which spirit, not matter, is again the primary reality.

I would like to thank once again the Bollingen Foundation for the generous Fellowship, twice renewed, which enabled me to undertake and to complete my work on Blake; and also Girton College, Cambridge, where these lectures and much of the larger book, *Blake and Tradition*, were written.

London, February 1977   KATHLEEN RAINE

LIST OF ILLUSTRATIONS

The following sources of photographs are abbreviated: Library of Congress, Washington, D.C., Rosenwald Collection; National Gallery of Art, Washington, D.C., Rosenwald Collection; John R. Freeman and Co., London. The illustrations are located at the back of the book following the Select Bibliography.

THE CAVE OF THE NYMPHS

In 1947 Arlington Court in Devonshire was taken over by the National Trust; and among the broken glass and rubbish on top of a pantry cupboard was found one of Blake's most beautiful paintings, the tempera provisionally named by Mr. Kerrison [1] Preston "The Sea of Time and Space" (a phrase taken from one of Blake's letters), also known as "The Cycle of the Life of Man." It is clearly dated 1821, six years before Blake's death.

The subject of the painting might have been discovered long ago but for the widespread misunderstanding of Blake's "visions." "The Nature of my Work is Visionary or Imaginative," he wrote; but vision is not hallucination, it is imaginative insight; nature he called one continued vision of imagination. Not only did he consider the Bible a work of vision but also the writings of Milton, Shakespeare, Ovid, and Apuleius, the paintings of Dürer, Fra Angelico, Constable. Nearly the whole of ancient art must be called, in Blake's sense, "Visionary or Imaginative." He would have accepted Yeats's definition of poetry as "the traditional expression of certain heroic and religious themes, passed on from age to age, modified by individual genius, but never abandoned." Yeats, indeed, might have recognized Blake's subject; for not in spite of but because of the visionary nature of his art Blake was, in an age of individualism, naturalism, and humanism, a traditional artist.

But we are able to recognize only what we are qualified to discover; and if, instead of regarding Blake—against the testimony of his friends to his enormous reading and great knowledge of the art of all periods—as an untaught original, we look in his work for the unchanging themes of the imaginative tradition, we shall make strange discoveries.

It has been held that because in this painting we find so many of the symbols that appear again and again in Blake's writings it must be an illustration of his own mythology; and so it is. But this single work provides enough evidence to compel us to reverse the argument: the basic symbols of his own visions we find to be traditional.

The first scholar to suggest Blake's debt to the neo-Platonists was Foster Damon; *William Blake: His Philosophy and Symbols* laid the foundations of modern Blake studies, and was followed by another distinguished American contribution, Milton O. Percival's *William Blake's Circle of Destiny*. Since these lectures were written, George Mills Harper's *The Neoplatonism of William Blake* has confirmed their findings and some of my own. But even now the importance of this debt has not been fully grasped, perhaps because it cannot be understood in academic terms alone.

Neo-Platonism may be compared to an underground river that flows through European history, sending up, from time to time, springs and fountains; and wherever its fertilizing stream emerges, there imaginative thought revives, and we have a period of great art and poetry. The works that taught Blake and the other English Romantic poets are the same that inspired the Florentine School of Athens, the American Transcendentalists, and in our own lifetime laid the foundations of the Irish renaissance; many of the works Blake studied are on the shelves of William Butler Yeats's library, in Dublin, to this day.

Blake knew little Greek; but as a young man he knew Thomas Taylor the Platonist, who called himself "the English Plethon," and who was called "the English Pagan." Professor Damon identified him as a character in Blake's early burlesque *An Island in the Moon*, "Sipsop the Pythagorean." Like Taylor, Sipsop was an enthusiast for "the Ancients." It is not always clear who these were, but a respect for tradition, in its original purity, was evidently intended; and a generation later Blake's disciples Palmer, Calvert, Richmond, and their friends were to call themselves, from the Surrey village where they lived, "the Shoreham ancients," another gesture to tradition.

Taylor was ridiculed, even persecuted, for bringing to the attention of his age a philosophy so subversive to established values; for the Augustan view of "the classics" could not survive the translation of Plato into English. The *Edinburgh Review* published a thirty-two page attack upon Taylor's *Plato*, pouring scorn on Proclus and Plotinus; and the *Timaeus*, according to the Lowland Scots, was written only to expose the absurdity of the metaphysical system it sets forth. Horace Walpole in a private letter said outright what the Augustans really thought, that Plato was nonsense. But the tide was flowing; Coleridge delighted in Taylor's works, Shelley possessed them, Keats too reflected their influence; crossing the Atlantic, they were all-important in the American Transcendentalist movement. To Emerson and Bronson Alcott Taylor was, as George Russell and his friends later called him, "the uncrowned king."

In 1787 Blake was thirty and Taylor twenty-nine years old; Blake was writing *An Island in the Moon*, and Taylor had published his first translation, Plotinus' *Concerning the Beautiful*. Taylor's first *Hymns of Orpheus* appeared in the same year, and in 1788 Proclus' *Mathematical Commentaries*, together with an essay *On the Restoration of the Platonic Theology by the Later Platonists*, a summary of the essentials of Platonism and an impassioned apologia for the author's own philosophy; in this essay and in his other early writings, Taylor called upon the "young men of the new age" to enlist under the banner of Plotinus, confident that "the weapons of truth, in the hands of vigorous union, descend with irresistible force, and are fatal wherever they fall." Was Blake for a time a convert to Taylor's Platonic revival? Or was Taylor's enthusiasm caught from Blake, who, inspired by Swedenborg, was also proclaiming that "A new heaven has begun"? However that may be, Blake knew this essay; for it contains a translation of the work of which the painting, whose theme has remained for so long a mystery, is an illustration: Porphyry's *De Antro Nympharum* (Cave of the Nymphs). As Blake grew older he moved towards a more explicit Christianity; but this picture, painted with such evident love, such wealth of symbolic detail, makes it plain that he never disowned the philosophy that had given him the basis of his own symbolism.

The nymphs, the weavers at their loom, the sea-god, those radiant spirits reborn in their everlasting youth from Blake's imagination, are age-old. They enact the perpetual cycle of the descent and return of souls between an eternal and a temporal world. Of this journey, the voyage of Odysseus, his sufferings and adventures, his departure and his homecoming to Ithaca, was, for the neo-Platonists, the type and symbol. The central figure is Odysseus, who has reached after his long wanderings his native shore, in the cove of the sea-god Phorcys, close to the Cave of the Nymphs. He is in the act of throwing something out to sea, but with his face averted; and in this gesture lies the clue to his identity. Blake has combined the two accounts of the hero's coming safe to land, the return to Ithaca and an episode from Book V of the *Odyssey*, the shipwreck on Phaeacia. Odysseus is the only survivor; for the goddess Ino, or Leucothea, takes pity on him, lends him her girdle, and urges him to swim for the shore; she tells him that when he comes to land he must throw it

[2] back to her, far out to sea, *turning his face away*. This episode Blake has shown; Odysseus has thrown the girdle, the goddess has caught it, and it is dissolving back into a spiral of radiant cloud.

The female figure who stands behind Odysseus, pointing to the shining realm of the sun, is Athene, depicted not with hel-

[4] met and Gorgon-shield, but as the figure of the Divine Wisdom, somewhat like the Beatrice of the Dante illustrations, painted soon after.

The sea, and water, in the ancient world, was always taken as a symbol of matter, because of its continual flux: a symbol retained in the Christian rite of baptism. Blake's phrase "the Sea of Time & Space" is itself a description of that symbol, well known to him from many sources. Of Odysseus and his voyage Thomas Taylor had written at length not only in a long footnote to his translation of Porphyry, but in *Concerning the Beautiful*, and in his *Hymns of Orpheus*. The watery cave of Calypso, he says, is the world and its enchantments; Odysseus, in his long captivity and desire for home, is the type of the soul on earth who inwardly pines for his native country, the eternal world. The beggar's rags in which the hero at last returns are the body, which the soul throws away when no longer needed. No doubt the author of "The Rime of the Ancient Mariner," who as a schoolboy delighted in the writings of the English Pagan, also knew these passages. Blake himself often writes of the body and its memories as "rotten rags"; but in this painting the discarding of the body is implied in the sea-garment melting into cloud—Blake's usual symbol for the physical body.

> And these black bodies and this sunburnt face
> Is but a cloud, . . .

—so he wrote in "The Little Black Boy"; the child in the "Intro-
[3] duction" to *Songs of Innocence*, "On a cloud"; and the weeping babe of *Songs of Experience*, "Like a fiend hid in a cloud." The moist cloud

as a symbol of the body is used also by the neo-Platonists, who describe the souls who come into generation attracting to themselves a watery envelope.

The symbolism of the sea-voyage constantly reappears in English poetry: in the sea-crossing of the second book of *The Faerie Queene*, in "The Rime of the Ancient Mariner," in Shelley's "Witch of Atlas"; and Yeats paraphrased Taylor's translation of the Delphic Oracle upon Plotinus, the type of the enlightened soul who comes within sight of our native country, eternity.

I have digressed only to remind you that the symbolic language of neo-Platonism is a thread woven throughout European art and poetry; the language may at times be forgotten, yet we cannot call it dead; for the visions it describes are, as Blake says, "Permanent in The Imagination"; the beauty and the meaning of such symbols is unaging.

But here it is necessary to give the text of Homer which prefaces Porphyry's treatise *De Antro Nympharum* and forms the theme of Blake's painting. I give Thomas Taylor's translation:

> High at the head a branching olive grows,
> And crowns the pointed cliffs with shady boughs.
> A cavern pleasant, though involv'd in night,
> Beneath it lies, the Naiades' delight.
> Where bowls and urns of workmanship divine
> And massy beams in native marble shine;
> On which the Nymphs amazing webs display,
> Of purple hue, and exquisite array.
> The busy bees, within the urns secure
> Honey delicious, and like nectar pure.
> Perpetual waters through the grotto glide,
> And lofty gates unfold on either side;
> That to the north is previous to mankind;
> The sacred south t'immortals is consign'd.

Porphyry says that the Cave of the Nymphs was no invention of Homer's, and that such caves have been from very ancient times sacred to the female powers. A cave, or den, he says, is a symbol of the world; and he quotes from Plato's *Republic* the famous passage that describes mankind as dwelling in a cavern where only shadows of real things are seen. He speaks of the temples of Mithra which were, like Porphyry's cave, grottos watered by springs and fountains. The world, says Porphyry, is very lovely, indeed, to him who first enters into it, but obscure to him who surveys its foundation, and examines it with an "intellectual eye," . . . so that its exterior and superficial parts are pleasant, but its interior and profound parts are obscure, and its very bottom is darkness itself.

This beautiful but awe-inspiring image of the material world Blake used continually; the senses are the "five windows" that light "the cavern'd Man" through "narrow chinks of his cavern." A great part of *The Four Zoas* tells of the exploration of "the [5] caverns of the Grave," and the "dens" of spiritual darkness, by which he means this present world.

From the secret depths water perpetually flows, and, like Alph the Sacred River, runs "through caverns measureless to man," down to the sunless sea of matter: sunless because remote from spiritual light and, as Blake shows it, storm-tossed. This same river-source of life in the depths of a cave is described in the Orphic "Hymn to the Fates," who, like the Naiades, dwell where "the waters of the heavenly lake"

> Burst from a fountain hid in depths of night
> And through a dark and stony cavern glide,
> A cave profound, invisible.

On this authority, no doubt, Blake has introduced the Fates into his composition.

The small figure of a nymph pouring water from an urn and

the reclining lovers near her are an emblem of the source of all life. "What's water but the generated soul?" Yeats asks, in a line that summarizes the teaching of the Platonists; for "souls descending into generation," it is said, "fly to moisture." Heraclitus said that "a dry soul is the wisest"; but also that "moisture appears delightful to souls," although it is deadly to them, since birth into the cave is a death from eternity, the sleep of forgetfulness that overcomes those who, as in Plato's parable, drink the waters of Lethe and are born on earth. "Let, therefore, the present cavern be consecrated to souls, and to nymphs that preside over streams and fountains, and who, on this account, are called fontal, and Naiades." So Porphyry concludes his exposition of the world cave. It is the womb by which man enters life.

There could be no fitter symbol of the identity and ambiguity [6] of womb and tomb than those "bowls and urns of workmanship divine" which Blake has represented carried on the heads, in the manner of water-pots, of winged nymphs in the deepest recess of the cave. These nymphs are Porphyry's bees, who deposit their honey in "bowls and urns." The bees are souls, still winged, about to descend into the cave of the world by way of these womb-like urns—"the Funeral Urns of Beulah," they become in Blake's myth, for Beulah is a Biblical symbol of marriage; by "Funeral Urns" Blake signifies that to enter the womb is to die from eternity.

[7]   The looms of generation appear continually in Blake's poems;
[8] [9] all his female figures are weavers of garments; and when he painted this picture he had his own work behind him; so that in the weaving nymphs we may recognize his own Daughters of Albion, whose shuttles are plied with such cruel delight to bind the eternals into mortal bodies. He had found this symbol long ago in Porphyry, who writes that "to souls that descend into generation, what symbol can be more appropriate than the instruments of weaving?" Homer writes of marble looms and purple garments: "for the formation of the flesh is on or about

the bones, which in the bodies of animals resemble stones. Hence the instruments of weaving consist of stone; but the purple webs are evidently the flesh, which is woven from blood . . . Add, too, that the body is a garment with which the soul is invested, a thing wonderful to the sight."

The little girl on the right of the looms is enmeshed in what the nymphs are weaving; she is being woven into the garment of the body.

Like the symbols of sea and cave, this symbolism of weaving is age-old. In 1793 or '94 (we know he had at that time already read Porphyry) Blake illustrated a poem by Thomas Gray, based on an episode from the Orkney saga. A man from Caithness saw twelve weird women enter a hollow hill. "Curiosity led him to follow them"—so Gray retells the story—"till looking through an opening in the rocks he saw twelve gigantic figures resembling women; they were all employed about a loom, and as they wove, they sang"; and their song, as Gray wrote it, Blake illustrated by a group of three female figures who are weaving a battlefield from the entrails of kings and warriors:

> See the griesly texture grow!
[10] > ('Tis of human entrails made)
> And the weights, that play below,
> Each a gasping Warriour's head.
>
> Shafts for shuttles, dipt in gore,
> Shoot the trembling cords along,
> Sword, that once a Monarch bore.
> Keep the tissue close and strong.

There is a suggestion of this group of three figures in Blake's composition, and something of their cruelty in the expression of the weaving nymphs—as there is in nearly every reference to the weavers of bodies in Blake's poems.

> Thou, Mother of my Mortal part,
> With cruelty didst mould my Heart. . . .

Much that is obscure in Blake's writings becomes clear as we begin to learn his symbolic terms. In *The Gates of Paradise* "weary Man"—the soul sinking into a phase of death or sleep—finds *garments* in a *cave*, and these are garments of death; the Christian theme of the Incarnation is grafted onto Porphyry's myth:

> When weary Man enters his Cave
> He meets his Saviour in the Grave
> Some find a Female Garment there,
> And some a Male, woven with care,
> Lest the Sexual Garments sweet
> Should grow a devouring Winding sheet.

Here the world-cave is the grave "where the Dead dwell," and the Saviour himself puts on the body of death. Blake sometimes writes of the people of this world as "sleepers," those "sunk in deadly sleep," or "the Spectres of the Dead," for death, in this symbolic sense, is only a deeper oblivion.

Stranger still, unless we remember that "the formation of the flesh is on . . . the bones, which in . . . animals resemble stones," are Blake's images of *stone* looms on which the females weave their garments.

> . . . and they drew out from the Rocky Stones
> Fibers of Life to Weave, for every Female is a Golden Loom,
> The Rocks are opake hardness covering all Vegetated things;
> And they Wove & Cut from the Looms, in various divisions . . .
> They divided into many lovely Daughters, to be counterparts
> To those they Wove; . . .
> > . . . in opake hardness

> They cut the Fibres from the Rocks: groaning in pain they
>   Weave,
> Calling the Rocks Atomic Origins of Existence, denying
>   Eternity. . . .

—for the weaving of souls into bodily garments is a denial of the soul's winged eternal nature. Blake's obscurities are never vague; they are hard, precise, and insoluble until we have the key to their meaning; they then vanish altogether. Thus, in an even stranger image, he writes, in *Jerusalem*,

> . . . they cut the fibres from the Rivers; he sears them with hot
> Iron of his Forge & fixes them into Bones of chalk & Rock.
> Conwenna sat above; with solemn cadences she drew
> Fibres of life out from the Bones into her golden Loom. . . .
> For the Male is a Furnace of beryll, the Female is a golden
>   Loom.

Two figures in the right foreground provide visible evidence that Blake was working not merely from Homer but from Porphyry; for of them there is no mention in Homer's text. They illustrate the parable of the tubs, from the *Gorgias*; Socrates tells how the temperate soul possesses a full tub, whereas the soul overcome by passion is like a pierced tub that can never be filled. Porphyry also quotes Hesiod, who speaks of one tub closed, the other opened by pleasure, who scatters its contents everywhere. These two conditions Blake has illustrated by two women. One, sober and resolute, has turned her back on the swirling waters and begun to climb the steps of the cave, against the current of generation. In her right hand she carries her bucket, while her left is raised towards the heavenly world. She is beginning the journey of re-ascent; and she is opposed by the nymphs, for she is a "dry soul" and her purpose is contrary to their nature and function.

Close to her, in the right foreground, the uninitiated soul, dominated by desire, lies sunk in her "deadly sleep." She is half immersed in the water, reclining over her tub, which lies on its side, the water lapping into it, forever unfilled. Her expression is one of bliss and unconsciousness; for she is a "moist soul," proceeding on her downward journey to the sea.

The looms of generation passed, we reach the lowest stage of the descent into matter, the troubled waters of the river's mouth where the Fates control the entry of souls into "the Sea of Time & Space." With faces of savage cruelty and joy, one unwinds the thread from a great distaff hung with flax; a second measures off [11] the yarn; and the third holds the shears that cut the thread. Phorcys is but a variant of Proteus, the Old Man of the Sea who is so slippery to hold because he has the power of changing his shape. This god is, according to tradition, (Bacon mentions this meaning) a symbol of that universal shape-shifter matter; and it is appropriate, therefore, that he bears the phallic distaff from which the Fates are spinning. The seemingly arbitrary combination of weaving with river and sea, found in a passage from Milton, falls into place when we consider that from the looms of the cave souls are washed down into the waters of the bay of Phorcys:

> . . . Tirzah & her Sisters
> Weave the black Woof of Death. . . .
> . . . they sing to the winged shuttle.
> The River rises above his banks to wash the Woof:
> He takes it in his arms; he passes it in strength thro' his
>   current;
> The veil of human miseries is woven over the Ocean
> From the Atlantic to the Great South Sea, the Erythrean.

—the "red sea" of lifeblood.

What of the flames that pour out of the cave, on the right of the painting, close to the looms? The symbol is a familiar one in Blake's poems: "The Male is a Furnace of beryll; the Female is a golden Loom." Wherever the looms are, there too are the furnaces. There is no mention of fire in Homer, nor in Porphyry. But those poets who employ the strict language of tradition do not invent symbols; nor has Blake done so.

[12] Porphyry speaks of the temples of Mithras as belonging to the cult of the cave; but Blake was familiar with Mithraic temples long before Taylor's Porphyry was published. He had worked, as [13] an apprentice to the engraver Basire, on the plates for Jacob Bryant's *Analysis of Antient Mythology*, the *Golden Bough* of its day. Bryant has a great deal to say about Mithraic temples; he quotes from Porphyry—of whom Blake must have learned for the first time in Bryant—but he stresses especially the worship of fire in caves. A number of his plates illustrate this fire-worship. What, then, could be more natural than that Blake, wishing to make, in his painting a complete symbolic statement of the cult of the Cave, should introduce this fire?

So much for the downward path; but there are two gates to the cave, one for mortals, the other for immortals; one for the souls who descend, the other for souls returning to the eternal world. Porphyry relates them to the Zodiac: the northern gate, through which the souls descend, is Cancer; the southern gate of return, Capricorn. "The sun and moon," Porphyry writes, "are the gates of souls, which ascend through the sun, and descend through the moon." The bright spirits round the sun's chariot are the immortal souls.

The nature of the alternate phases is suggested in the contrasting characters of the figures of the two worlds. In contrast with the fierce activity of the descending path, the sun-god in his chariot is sunk in profound sleep; for when this world wakes, the other sleeps; it becomes, in terms of modern psychology, unconscious.

[14] The god in the chariot of the sun is a strange figure. He does

not resemble the traditional Apollo; he has no bow of burning gold; but he does strikingly resemble the figure of God in the *Job* engravings; and in the fifth plate of *Job*, also, we see the god becoming drowsy, though not actually sleeping. The symbolic [15] event is parallel; for the separation of Satan, the human selfhood, from the divine world is about to activate just such a cycle of Experience as the Platonic lapse of the soul. Job's sufferings, like the voyage of Odysseus, commence when there is a loss of the vision of eternity, here represented by the god within. We may think, also, of the opening lines of *The Gates of Paradise*,

> My Eternal Man set in Repose,
> [16]   The Female from his darkness rose. . . .

Here again the falling asleep of "the Eternal Man" initiates a descent into the cave or grave of mortal life, a falling into the power of the females, and a putting on of their garments; the Traveller, like Odysseus, at last returns to his native land:

> But when once I did descry
> The Immortal Man that cannot Die,
> Thro' evening shades I haste away
> To close the Labours of my Day.

Man returns to life through the door of death. This cycle of descent and return, the journey of the Traveller who leaves his native country and returns to it again, is not Christian, it is Platonic; and even into his interpretation of *Job* Blake is carrying that grand conception that re-echoes from Heraclitus down through the Greek philosophers and poets, "we live their death, and we die their life." But the sun as the symbol of deity unites Christian and classical symbolism. Swedenborg's angels saw the Lord as the Sun, made up of a countless multitude of souls; and when Blake wrote that when he saw the sun he saw "an

Innumerable company of the Heavenly host crying, 'Holy, Holy, Holy is the Lord God Almighty,'" his "vision" included all [17] these. His painting of "The River of Life," illustrating a passage in the Book of Revelation, shows souls travelling down the river towards that same spirit-encompassed sun; here the figure with the shear is the same as the Fate who cuts the thread of life. This painting communicates, in other terms, the same vision, the return of all souls to

> ... that sweet golden clime
> Where the traveller's journey is done.

THE MYTH OF PSYCHE

The first evidence of Blake's reading of Porphyry appears in *The Book of Thel*, written in 1787, thirty-two years before he painted the Arlington tempera. In the early *Poetical Sketches* we already find many traces of his wide reading, but only in a sense that may be called literary. *Songs of Innocence* already speak a symbolic language; but their themes, many of them drawn from Swedenborg, are on a small scale. That strange poem "Tiriel" is a hybrid; it represents the first impact of the Greek revival upon Blake, but here a Greek theme—the story of Oedipus—is grafted onto Gothic symbolism, derived from Swedenborg, Cornelius Agrippa, and Norse myths. But once Blake had set his soul to study in a learned school, with Thomas Taylor and the Platonic philosophers, he quickly became master of a coherent symbolic system which he handled with ever-increasing scope and freedom.

Not only did neo-Platonism give him a vocabulary and grammar of symbolic terms; it placed him in the mainstream of European poetic and pictorial symbolism. From his reading of

Porphyry and Plotinus he came to recognize in the works of poets already known to him the same symbols, endlessly recreated and re-clothed in beautiful forms. Thus he was able to extend his field of allusion and to introduce themes and images taken from many sources, without destroying the unity of his symbolic structure.

The Book of Thel is the first of the series of myths Blake wrote on the Platonic theme of the descent of the soul, each more complex than the last.

Thel is an ungenerated soul who looks down into mortal life; she sees "the land of clouds thro' valleys dark," "list'ning to the voices of the ground" that come from those who have "died" from the eternal into the temporal world. She asks the question the neo-Platonists leave unanswered: why should the soul descend? Thel is one of those "dry souls" called wise by Heraclitus, for she sees no good reason why the soul should take on a body;

> "Why a Tongue impress'd with honey from every wind?
> Why an Ear, a whirlpool fierce to draw creations in?
> Why a Nostril wide inhaling terror, trembling, & affright?
> Why a tender curb upon the youthful burning boy?
> Why a little curtain of flesh on the bed of our desire?"

We have evidence that Blake already knew The Cave of the Nymphs, for he refers to the northern gate of the cave, through which souls descend into generation:

> The eternal gates' terrific porter lifted the northern bar:
> Thel enter'd in & saw the secrets of the land unknown.
> She saw the couches of the dead, . . .

—those who are "dead" or "asleep" to eternity. But Blake's imagination is already weaving into the pattern new elements.

We know, from some early stanzas in imitation of *The Faerie Queene*, how greatly Blake admired Spenser; and he has in *Thel* clothed Porphyry's symbolic bones in Spenserian images. The very theme of the poem—mutability, and its mood of gentle lamentation, is Spenserian; and Blake recognized in Spenser another version of the Platonic theme of the Cave of the Nymphs, with its gates of life and death;

> The one of yron, the other of bright gold, . . .
> By which both in and out men moten pas;
> Th'one faire and fresh, the other old and dride . . .

Spenser's gates are guarded by a porter, Genius, god of generation, a figure from whom Blake was to develop his own Urthona, keeper of the gates of birth and death:

> He letteth in, he letteth out to wend,
>   All that to come into the world desire;
>   A thousand thousand naked babes attend
>   About him day and night, which doe require,
>   That he with fleshly weedes would them attire.
>   Such as him list, such as eternall fate
>   Ordained hath, he clothes with sinfull mire,
>   And sendeth forth to liue in mortall state,
> Till they againe returne back by the hinder gate.

These are the unborn souls, in Porphyry's fable called the "people of dreams," gathered outside the galaxy. In Spenser, they await birth in the Garden of Adonis; and by "the river of Adona" the unborn Thel laments the transience of mortal life. The river is that ever-flowing stream of the nymphs; and Milton, himself a poet strict in his use of symbols, writes of Adonis, the mortal and perishing lover of Venus and parent of "vegetated" bodies, ever in flux, as a river.

> . . . smooth Adonis from his native rock
> Ran purple to the sea.

Thel's "river of Adona" combines Porphyry and Spenser.

> . . . by the river of Adona her soft voice is heard, . . .
> "O life of this our spring! why fades the lotus of the water,
> Why fade these children of the spring, born but to smile &
> fall?"

She is echoing Spenser's Venus, who is, like her, a lamenting figure:

> And their great mother *Venus* did lament
> The losse of her deare Brood, her dear delight:
> Her hart was pierst with pittie at the sight,
> When walking through the Gardin, them she spyde,
> Yet no'te she find redresse for such despight.
> For all that liues, is subject to that law:
> All things decay in time, and to their end do draw.

20]   The title-page shows Thel gravely watching the embrace of two small spirits of vegetation, who emerge from flowers that in most of the copies of this book are painted purple or red. They are the *anemone pulsatilla* into which Adonis was changed; and this emblem tells us the theme of the poem that follows, the mutability of generated life. A similar flower appears in *Songs of Inno-*
21] *cence*, illustrating the poem "Infant Joy"; within its crimson womb-like petals we see the Infant Joy, one of the "thousand thousand naked babes" who descend from the galaxy, tended by a spirit of vegetation.

22]   In an earlier drawing, from Blake's notebook, we again recognize the little female figure and the pursuing male that Thel is watching so thoughtfully as she "considers sexual generation."

Under the drawing Blake has written two lines from Shakespeare's fifteenth Sonnet:

> When I consider every thing that growes
>   Holds in perfection but a little moment. . . .

We begin to understand from what a rich context of associated themes Blake has recreated his poem; for the sonnet continues to reflect upon the theme of mutability:

> When I perceive that men as plants increase,
> Cheared and checkt even by the selfe-same skie,
> Vaunt in their youthfull sap, at height decrease. . . .

The flower is indeterminate—not, certainly, the anemone; that was an idea that flashed into Blake's mind later, from Spenser, giving him the minute particular form of Thel's "vision." A pair
[23] of lovers in a "lotus of the water" appear in *Jerusalem*, and in lilies in *The Song of Los*.

There are many other traces of Spenser's images in *Thel* and of Porphyry's images in Spenser; but one more is enough—the Lilly in *The Book of Thel* is

> ". . . clothed in light, and fed with morning manna,
> Till summer's heat melts thee beside the fountains and the
>   springs
> To flourish in eternal vales . . ."

—an image strictly traditional; for the fountains and springs are Porphyry's fountains of the nymphs, and the Lilly tells of a descent and return. Spenser uses the same image of evanescence:

> And that faire flowre of beautie fades away,
> As doth the lilly fresh before the sunny ray.

Spenser too writes of "eternal vales"; for the faded lillies return to the "first seminarie of all things,"

> And grow afresh, as they had neuer seene
> Fleshly corruption, nor mortall paine.

Blake's poem is filled with the "watery" imagery of Neo-Platonism. We have the river, the "lotus of the water," dewdrop, rainbow, and "wat'ry cloud." The Lilly calls herself "a wat'ry weed," for like the Narcissus of whom Plotinus writes in his tractate *Concerning the Beautiful*, she is a type of generated, or, as Blake more often says, of "vegetated" life. Cloud and dewdrop, the moist clay of the body, the worm upon its "dewy bed," and Thel's own "dewy grave" are images not descriptive only, or chiefly, of physical appearances, though they do at the same time build up an exquisite and coherent symbolic landscape. They are exact symbolic terms and describe, like Enion's "wat'ry Grave" in the poem *Vala*, the moist envelope of the soul, the generated body in which the soul is "dead" to eternity; the "bed" as the place of the soul's sleep, as it passes, in Plotinus' words, "from bed to bed, from sleep to sleep." All is appropriate to the theme of the "moist soul"; the whole poem is, like the world of Porphyry's nymphs, "drenched in moisture."

Plotinus' *Concerning the Beautiful* is likewise filled with imagery of shadows, reflections, and water that we find in *Thel*; and Taylor in a note quotes Proclus, who describes the forms which appear in matter as "merely ludicrous shadows falling upon shadows, as in a mirror where the position of a thing is different from its real situation. . . . The things which enter and depart from matter are nothing but imitations of being, and semblances, . . . like images in water, or as if anyone should fill a vacuum with forms." Thel uses these very images;

> "Ah! Thel is like a wat'ry bow, and like a parting cloud;
> Like a reflection in a glass; like shadows in the water;

> Like dreams of infants, like a smile upon an infant's face;
> Like the dove's voice; like transient day; like music in the air."

Thel is afraid that if she descends into generation she will exchange her immortal for a mortal nature:

> "And I complain'd in the mild air, because I fade away,
> And lay me down in thy cold bed, and leave my shining lot."

Why should the soul descend? The poem gives no answer; and Thel, appalled at the "secrets" of the grave that she has been permitted to see,

> ... with a shriek
> Fled back unhinder'd till she came into the vales of Har.

She is following the advice of Plotinus, to turn away quickly from the "profound and horrid darkness" of material life. "It is here, then, we may exclaim," Plotinus writes, "Let us depart from hence, and fly to our father's delightful land."

This "grave-plot" is an image that reappears in many of [24] Blake's early designs. The title-page of *Songs of Experience*, Gothic in style, is Platonic in content; for the "dead" mourned by the weeping females are those who have left eternity; and Blake has indicated, in placing this emblem at the beginning of these Songs of the mortal world, the condition of the souls whose stories are told in the poems that follow.

The unresolved question of Thel—what reason can be given for the descent of the soul—Blake took up again in an episode in the last Night of *The Four Zoas*; and again we find new strands woven into the design. These strengthen, but they do not confuse, the theme; for Blake works always from the symbolic bones, never from the accidents of mere imagery. The new myth added is the Fable of Cupid and Psyche. We know

Blake admired Apuleius; for he wrote that The Golden Ass and Ovid's Metamorphosis "contain Vision in a sublime degree, being derived from real Vision in More ancient Writings." We shall presently see what more ancient writing Blake divined behind The Golden Ass.

He probably read Apuleius' fable in Adlington's beautiful sixteenth-century translation when he was engraving some plates for a mutual friend of Thomas Taylor and himself. George Cumberland's Thoughts on Outline is one of the forgotten works of the seventeen-nineties in which we may see reflected the early enthusiasm of the Greek revival; and among Cumberland's plates [25] were several illustrating the story of Cupid and Psyche. Meanwhile, in 1795, Taylor had published his own translation of the fable, with an introduction explaining its symbolism.

Another author of the time who had fallen under the spell of Greek mythology was Erasmus Darwin. In his notes to The Botanic Garden he writes that the myth of Cupid and Psyche formed part of the Eleusinian Mysteries; and he describes the butterfly as the emblem of the soul—an emblem which Blake too uses, [26] especially of Vala, the soul figure of his later books.

The story of Cupid and Psyche tells of a king's daughter who by a divine decree must be married to a serpent. She is led to the summit of a mountain by her mourning "parents," who see her no more. They believe her dead; but she is carried safely down to [27] a valley, where "near the fall of a river"—we recognize the place—she finds a house prepared for her. There she is visited by a divine lover, who remains invisible. She is led to doubt the god, who thereupon leaves her; and only after long wanderings and the performance of laborious tasks does the soul reascend into the world of the gods.

We recognize the familiar theme of descent and return; Psyche's marriage, like the descent of souls in Porphyry's myth, is described as a kind of death; for when she leaves her native country "the maid that should be married did wipe her eyes with her veile . . . and they went to bring this sorrowfull spowse, not to her marriage but to her finale end and buriale." Her [28] marriage-veil is her bodily garment, with which she is vested for her descent into generation.

Vala, in the poem that bears her name, makes the descent Thel refused; and her figure is enriched by attributes of Psyche. She too comes to the Northern Gate, and the porter admits her; but she does not enter the world alone: she is accompanied by a divine lover who has prepared a garden for her. Blake's Luvah, in the first appearance of this theme, tells of his love for Vala, "the sinless soul":

> "I loved her, I gave her all my soul & my delight,
> I hid her in soft gardens & in secret bowers of summer,
> Weaving mazes of delight along the sunny paradise. . . ."

He leads her into the earthly paradise, a paradise of shadows, for, as Plato himself taught, earth is but a shadow of eternity:

> Luvah & Vala descended & enter'd the Gates of Dark Urthona,
> And walk'd from the hands of Urizen in the shadows of Vala's
>   Garden
> Where the impressions of Despair & Hope for ever vegetate
> In flowers, in fruits, in fishes, birds & beasts & clouds & waters,
> The land of doubts & shadows, sweet delusions, unform'd
>   hopes.

But we presently discover Vala seeking among the shadows of her garden, "Weeping for Luvah lost"; and soon after, like Psyche, toiling at hard tasks, in exile:

> Thus she lamented day & night, compell'd to labour & sorrow.

Blake has adapted the essential details of Apuleius' fable to his account of Vala's "lower paradise." Like Psyche she is carried to her valley in sleep; like her she wakes to find herself the mistress of a house. Apuleius' description of Psyche's Graeco-Roman house built for her by Cupid has delighted many poets beside Blake:

> . . . well nigh at the fall of the river was a princely Edifice, wrought and builded not by the art or hand of man, but by the mighty power of God: and you would judge at the first entry therein, that it were some pleasant and worthy mansion for the powers of heaven. For the embowings above were Citron and Ivory, propped and undermined with pillars of gold, the walls covered and seeled with silver, divers sort of beasts were graven and carved, that seemed to encounter with such as entered in. All things were so curiously and finely wrought that it seemed either to be the work of some Demygod, or of God himselfe. The pavement was all of pretious stones, divided and cut one from another, whereon was carved divers kinds of pictures, in such sort that blessed and thrice blessed were they which might goe upon such a pavement: Every part and angle of the house was so well adorned, that by reason of the pretious stones and inestimable treasure there, it glittered and shone in such sort, that the chambers, porches, and doores gave out light as it had been the Sunne.

Vala's house too is by a river; and in it we find Apuleius' pillars of gold and walls of ivory; and the mosaic pavement, "all of pretious stones," becomes in Blake a "pavement as of pearl"—neither Adlington nor Blake had seen one. This house is the body into which the soul enters when in "sleep" she descends from eternity:

> And soft sleep fell upon her eyelids in the silent noon of day.
> Then Luvah passed by, & saw the sinless soul,

And said: "Let a pleasant house arise to be the dwelling place
Of this immortal spirit growing in lower Paradise."
He spoke, & pillars were builded, & walls as white as ivory.
The grass she slept upon was pav'd with pavement as of pearl.
Beneath her rose a downy bed, & a cieling cover'd all.

Vala awoke. "When in the pleasant gates of sleep I enter'd,
I saw my Luvah like a spirit stand in the bright air.
Round him stood spirits like me, who rear'd me a bright house,
And here I see thee, house, remain in my most pleasant world.
My Luvah smil'd: I kneeled down: he laid his hand on my head,
And when he laid his hand upon me, from the gates of sleep I
    came
Into this bodily house to tend my flocks in my pleasant
    garden."

Psyche, on awakening in her valley, bathes before she ascends
her marriage bed; and Vala too descends into the river before her
consciousness can become attuned to the world of matter, as
Plato describes the souls passing through the river Lethe—
matter—before they enter mortal life. Vala, like these, "stop'd to
drink of the clear spring. . . ."

Thel thought herself "an image in the wat'ry glass," and
describes herself as

"Like a reflection in a glass; like shadows in the water. . . ."

But Vala is wiser; she realizes that body is only the reflection or
shadow of the soul cast in the "river" of matter:

She stood in the river & *view'd* herself within the wat'ry
    glass, . . .

—without identification with the image. Like Psyche, Vala is attended, in her bodily house, by invisible servants. These are the spiritual agents of all natural appearances; "for," so Blake believed, "every Natural Effect has a Spiritual Cause." But it is not only her servants who are invisible to her; it is the divine lover himself. As Psyche could hear the voice of Cupid though she could not see him, so Vala hears the voice of Luvah:

> Invisible Luvah in bright clouds hover'd over Vala's head,
> And thus their ancient golden age renew'd, for Luvah spoke

—and he calls Vala to "Rise from the dews of death. . . ." She answers,

> "Whose voice is this, in the voice of the nourishing air,
> In the spirit of the morning, awaking the Soul from its grassy bed?
> Where dost thou dwell? for it is thee I seek, & but for thee I must have slept Eternally. . . ."

All follows as in the old legend; for it is Cupid, when after her last task Psyche has fallen into a deadly sleep, who awakens her, and raises her among the gods to "make her his eternal bride"; and Vala returns as the bride of Luvah to Blake's "sweet golden clime," saying, as Porphyry's souls might say,

> "To yonder brightness, there I haste, for sure I came from thence . . ."

Blake has written this episode in order to give the answer Thel failed to find: it is not the soul that is fleeting, but the world. Vala's divine lover calls to her:

> "Rise, sluggish soul, why sit'st thou here? why dost thou sit & weep?

> Yon sun shall wax old & decay, but thou shalt ever flourish.
> The fruit shall ripen & fall down, & the flowers consume away,
> But thou shalt still survive; arise, O dry thy dewy tears."

—and she answers:

> "Hah! shall I still survive? whence came that sweet & comfort-
> ing voice? . . .
> O that I could behold his face & follow his pure feet!
> I walk by the footsteps of his flocks; come hither, tender flocks.
> Can you converse with a pure soul that seeketh for her maker?"

Vala is often described as a shepherdess; she

> . . . laid her head on the downy fleece
> [29] Of a curl'd Ram who stretch'd himself in sleep beside his
> mistress,
> And soft sleep fell upon her eyelids in the silent noon of day.

Here we begin to notice traces of the "older writing" that Blake, with his genius in the reading of symbols, divined behind the fable of Cupid and Psyche.

When we read of the soul seeking "for her maker" we are no longer in the world of Greek mythology. The ram as an image of God comes not from Greece but from the Middle East; and with a line that precedes the scene above—

> "Where dost thou flee, O fair one? where dost thou seek thy
> happy place?"

—we recognize an echo from another love story of the soul: the *Song of Solomon*. Blake, with his perception of the essence of myths, saw that the story of Solomon and the fair Shulamite describes the same spiritual events as the Classical legend, the soul's love for the divine beloved, and God's love for the soul.

The two stories are so similar that it is not always possible to say upon which Blake is drawing; for, in the Hebrew poem also, the lovers are at first united; then (for no stated reason) the woman is abandoned, and must seek for her beloved throughout the city, in sorrow; and the speech of the Shulamite might be Psyche herself speaking after Cupid's flight from her marriage-bed:

> By night on my bed I sought him whom my soul loveth: I sought him, but I found him not.
>
> I will rise now, and go about the city in the streets, and in the broad ways I will seek him whom my soul loveth: I sought him, but I found him not.
>
> The watchmen that go about the city found me: to whom I said, Saw ye him whom my soul loveth?

So the Shulamite, like "Vala the sweet wanderer," becomes an exile seeking her lover. The parallel with Psyche's story is even closer in another passage, from which it seems the lover has departed in displeasure, or from some hidden necessity:

> I opened to my beloved; but my beloved had withdrawn himself, and was gone: my soul failed when he spake: I sought him, but I could not find him; I called him, but he gave me no answer.

There is even a suggestion that he becomes, like Cupid, invisible:

> O my dove, that art in the clefts of the rock, in the secret places of the stairs, let me see thy countenance, let me hear thy voice; for sweet is thy voice, and thy countenance is comely.

The identity of Luvah is unmistakable in the lines

> "Where is the voice of God that call'd me from the silent dew?
> Where is the Lord of Vala? dost thou hide *in clefts of the rock?*
> Why shouldst thou hide thyself from Vala, from the soul that
> wanders desolate?"

It is "the voice of God" who is "the Lord of Vala."

The "bodily house" is another symbol uniting the two legends; for in the *Song of Solomon* also, a house is built round the beloved—prototype of the "Turris eburnea domus aurea" of the Litany of the Blessed Virgin Mary:

> If she be a wall, we will build upon her a palace of silver: and
> if she be a door, we will inclose her with boards of cedar. I am a
> wall, and my breasts like towers: then was I in his eyes as one
> that found favour.

We may also remember King Solomon's chariot.

> He made the pillars thereof of silver, the bottom thereof of
> gold, the covering of it of purple, the midst thereof being paved
> with love, for the daughters of Jerusalem.

As the theme develops, Blake has added each new image without altering the structure and deepened, without ever changing, the meaning; the old myth has been, as it were, baptized. In [30] the final, and completely Christianized, version, in the poem *Jerusalem*, Blake has given the soul a Biblical name, one that links her incidentally with the Daughters of Jerusalem in the *Song of Solomon*.

There is in a poem in Blake's notebook another version of the bodily house, here called a chapel, but still recognizable as Psyche's mansion:

[19]   I saw a chapel all of gold
       That none did dare to enter in,
       And many weeping stood without,
       Weeping, mourning, worshipping.

       I saw a serpent rise between
       The white pillars of the door,
       And he forc'd & forc'd & forc'd,
       Down the golden hinges tore.

       And along the pavement sweet,
       Set with pearls & rubies bright
       All his slimy length he drew,
       Till upon the altar white

       Vomiting his poison out
       On the bread & on the wine.
       So I turn'd into a sty
       And laid me down among the swine.

Blake has here condensed in a few phrases the essence of the treasure-house that glittered and shone like the sun; the white pillars and golden hinges derive from the embowings of "Citron and Ivory, propped and undermined with pillars of gold"; and here again is the jewelled pavement. But now we have another symbol—the serpent, to whom the oracle of Apollo foretold Psyche's marriage:

     . . . serpent dire and fierce as might be thought
     Who flies with wings above in starry skies,
     And doth subdue each thing with firie flight.

With profound insight, the old myth recognizes the irresistible nature of Eros; and it recognizes another truth—that the god who to the sinless soul is beautiful, appears, in the fallen world, in a form of evil. Blake understood this too; for the beautiful and gentle Luvah becomes, in the "caves" and "dens" of experience, the serpent in the tree of life. Psyche's sisters tell her that the god whom she has married is in reality a loathesome serpent and advise her to murder him—advice often repeated in a world that sees in erotic love only its carnal form; and Psyche, through believing them, destroys her union with the divine beloved. In "I saw a chapel all of gold," Blake has told the degraded version of this myth of double aspect. This is not a good poem, and Blake did not include it in *Songs of Experience*; its interest lies, rather, in its relation to another poem written soon afterwards. In "The Sick Rose" we have the dire serpent, who flies in "starry skies," the lover and destroyer of the fallen soul; there are plenty of canker-worms in English poetry, but no other invisible, nocturnal, and flying worm:

[31]   O Rose, thou art sick!
         The invisible worm
         That flies in the night,
         In the howling storm,

         Has found out thy bed
         Of crimson joy:
         And his dark secret love
         Does thy life destroy.

So perfectly has Blake recreated his material, that, if it were not for the "chapel all of gold" written immediately before, and his return to the Cupid and Psyche story in *Vala*, we could scarcely discover, in the Invisible Worm, the legendary Eros.

So we are led back to that rich association of symbols linking the generation of the body, through the nymphs of marriage, with a death of the soul. Blake's powerful image, the *Marriage hearse*, in another poem, "London," summarizes in two words this profound paradox; and it may not be fanciful to recognize in this phrase, and in "The Sick Rose," an echo of Apuleius' description of Psyche's marriage, when "the pleasant songs were turned into pittifull cries, the melody of Hymenaeus was ended with deadly howling." The darkness, the black torches, the lamentations, and the supposed death of the bride, Blake conveys in three words, "the howling storm." With superb economy of symbol, but from a background of thought both rich and complex, "The Sick Rose" says everything that can ever be stated on this theme.

We recognize, in the little female fairy of "The Sick Rose," the design that came first to Blake when he illustrated Shakespeare's sonnet on mutability with a rapid pencil-sketch in his notebook, which he later adapted as the flower of Adonis in the Book of Thel; but here the male lover has become the worm, the defiler and destroyer, whose "dark secret love" brings the soul, through her marriage, to her death.

The rose-canker-worm symbolic association is so common in English poetry that it may seem unnecessary to look for a particular source; but since we know that the visual theme of "The Sick Rose" was first developed in illustrating Shakespeare's sonnet, may we not guess that his myth of rose and worm, so continuously used by Shakespeare as emblems of love and corruption, includes Blake's reflections on Shakespeare's view of love?

THE MYTH OF THE KORE
OR PERSEPHONE

The currents and cross-currents of fashion which lead a poet to the choice of his subjects tend to be forgotten, leaving some single work in isolation as if produced by chance or miracle. An example of this we find in the theme of the Grecian Urn, forever associated with Keats, but which had caught the imagination of artists a generation before. In about the year 1790 the Greek Revival was transforming English taste. Distinguished travellers were following the example of Lord Elgin, who had carried off the frieze of the Parthenon itself; and in a more modest way Sir William Hamilton, husband of Nelson's Lady Emma, made history, for it was he who brought to England the famous Barberini vase. Among those whom he invited to admire his treasure was the young sculptor Flaxman, then and for many years Blake's closest friend; and Flaxman, who designed for the Wedgwood pottery, wrote to Josiah Wedgwood urging him to come to London to "see Sir Wm. Hamilton's Vase, it is the finest production of Art brought to England"; he suggested that Wedgwood might make a replica. In 1786 the vase was purchased by the Duke of Portland, whose name it now bears, and four years later the Wedgwood pottery followed Flaxman's suggestion. The Wedgwood replica was exhibited at the Wedgwood show-rooms in London in 1790. Josiah Wedgwood himself lectured on the vase and on his replica. The next year Erasmus Darwin, a close friend [32] of the Wedgwoods, published, in the first part of his *Botanic Garden*, an essay on the vase, with a splendid set of engravings; and the engraver was William Blake—not surprisingly since Blake was a friend not only of Flaxman but of Johnson, Darwin's publisher; he worked from time to time, also, as an engraver for the Wedgwoods. The world was then, as now, a small one.

It is likely that Blake heard about the vase, and possibly saw it, when it belonged to Sir William Hamilton; it is more than likely that he visited the Wedgwood exhibition in Greek Street; it is certain that the magical object itself, or possibly the replica, was in his possession in the summer or autumn of 1791.

What was then being said about the vase—and no doubt discussed by Josiah Wedgwood in his lecture—must be presumed to be the view given by Erasmus Darwin in his essay. Perhaps because this is what those under the spell of Greece would have liked to be true, it was believed that the vase was a cult object of the Eleusinian Mysteries, and the figures depicted upon it emblems of the immortality of the soul, fittingly inscribed upon an urn designed to hold the ashes of the dead. Blake, himself under the spell, wrote two poems, first included in *Songs of Innocence* and later transferred to *Songs of Experience*, on the theme of the Mysteries and the figures on the vase. The Grecian Urn made its entry into English poetry with Blake.

"The Little Girl Lost" and "Found" tell the story of the Kore, whose death, or, as Blake says, "sleep," is watched with such grave wonder by the man and woman on the urn; and if we may guess what, in Blake's imagination, his own "Funeral Urns of Beulah" were like, we may not be wrong in imagining them as somewhat like the Portland Vase. It is said of the Daughters of Beulah (the Nymphs) that

> . . . the Eternal Promise
> They wrote on all their tombs & pillars, & on every Urn
> These words: "If ye will believe, your Brother shall rise again,"
> In golden letters ornamented with sweet labours of Love . . .

They were, in this, following the Graeco-Roman tradition that inscribed on urns and sarcophagi emblems of the mysteries of the Resurrection.

Meanwhile we may imagine how in that circle of young enthusiasts described by Blake in *An Island in the Moon*—Flaxman was among them, and Thomas Taylor—there was fine talk on a subject that must have delighted them all; and perhaps the Pythagorean was urged to write a book explaining to them these famous Mysteries. Be that as it may, Taylor did write such a book, his *Dissertation on the Eleusinian and Bacchic Mysteries*, published in 1789 or 1790—the date is uncertain. Many fantasias have been written on the old myths, some of them interesting in themselves, like those of Freud or Neumann; but Taylor interprets the symbols in the light of the philosophic tradition of which they formed a part—that is to say, correctly. The influence of this work on Blake's development as a maker of myths was profound and lasting.

When Blake incorporated a symbolic theme into his own mythology he was content with nothing less than complete mastery both of the minute particulars of image and of metaphysical content. He may have been pedantic: he was never imprecise; and when the Eleusinian Mysteries caught his imagination, he read everything available on the subject. Darwin describes the [33] first compartment of the Portland Vase as "an hieroglyphic or Eleusinian Emblem of Mortal Life." The maiden holds in her hand an inverted torch, emblem of death; she and the attendant figures who gravely watch her sit under a tree "which has not," as Darwin says, "the leaves of any evergreen of this climate, but may be supposed to be an elm, which Virgil places near the entrance of the infernal regions, and adds, that a dream was believed to dwell under every leaf of it." How completely the botanist Darwin must have been under the spell of the myth we can guess from his calling this tree an elm, which it quite obviously is not. Blake's Lyca, who invites death with the words

> "Sweet sleep, come to me
> Underneath this tree."

is this lovely recumbent maiden; and the man and woman— whom Darwin compares to Adam and Eve—are Lyca's "father" and "mother."

[34]   The emblem on the reverse side of the urn was said by Darwin to show the soul of the newly dead entering Hades, led by Love and welcomed by the king and queen of the underworld. The youthful figure of the initiate discards his garment as he enters—his "mortal dress," Darwin says, and the original, per- haps, of the "slender dress" of Lyca, Thel's "little curtain of flesh."

So far Darwin; but again the heart of Blake's thought is to be found in Taylor.

Taylor quotes a long passage from Sallust's treatise *On the Gods and the World* on the four kinds of meaning to be found in myths. First is their natural meaning—the story of Demeter and Perse- phone, for example, describes the rhythm of the seasons and crops; next is the psychological meaning; and beyond that the metaphysical or theological meaning, that tells, by analogy, of the nature of the cosmos itself. Sallust's fourth kind of myth is the mixed; and in most myths all these levels may be found. Sallust uses as an illustration the story of the Judgment of Paris;

and it may be more than coincidence that Blake painted this subject, introducing the figure of Eris, whom Sallust describes, but who does not commonly appear in paintings of this theme. In "A Little Girl Lost" and "Found" we see Blake using the myth of the Eleusinian mysteries, strictly observing the three levels distinguished by Sallust; Taylor not only gave him the story but taught him how to use it.

The story of the Mysteries tells how Persephone, daughter of Ceres and Jupiter, gathering spring flowers, was carried away by Pluto, through thick woods and over a length of sea, to a cavern, residence of departed spirits, over whom she afterwards ruled. But Ceres wandered over the whole earth looking for her daughter, finding her at last at Eleusis, where she taught the Eleusinians the mysteries of corn. This, in essence, is the story of Blake's poems "A Little Girl Lost" and "A Little Girl Found." Blake's little girl is Lyca; she is, like Persephone, at once the soul who "descends" into generation and, as we are told in the opening lines, the flowering earth:

> In futurity
> I prophetic see
> That the earth from sleep
> (Grave the sentence deep)
>
> Shall arise and seek
> For her maker meek;
> And the desart wild
> Become a garden mild.

The young Lyca of "A Little Girl Lost" is that same aged earth, "her locks cover'd with grey despair . . .," who is called, in the first poems of Songs of Experience, to awake from sleep and leave the cavern where she is "prison'd on wat'ry shore." The story of Lyca is of a descent into a cavern, a sleep, a search and discovery by her mother, and a foretold awakening. The first of the two poems tells the story of the Lesser Mysteries, the rape of Persephone; and the second, that of the Greater Mysteries, the wanderings of Demeter in search of her child.

Lyca's native home, like Persephone's, was

> In the southern clime,
> Where the summer's prime
> Never fades away,

—and we know from Porphyry that the South is the region of immortals. Blake is using this symbolism when in his account of the resurrection of the world, in *Vala* Night IX, he writes:

> The feast was spread in the bright South, & the Eternal Man
> Sat at the feast rejoicing. . . .

Like those souls irresistibly attracted towards generation, Lyca is
[36] overcome by a desire for sleep. Under the branches of a tree she invokes the powers of darkness, night, and the moon, all associated, as we know from Porphyry, with the descent of souls. Her first words express drowsiness:

> "Sweet sleep, come to me
> Underneath this tree."

The apparent naivety of the lines could not be more misleading, for the tree under which Lyca is lying is the elm, sacred to the god of sleep, that grows at the entrance to Hades, and that Darwin discovered on the Portland Vase. Virgil describes this tree in the Sixth Book of the *Aeneid*, which is generally considered to be a description of these same Mysteries; and Blake, if he found difficulty in reading the Latin Taylor quotes, probably turned to Dryden:

> Full in the midst of this infernal road,
> An elm displays her dusky arms abroad:
> The God of Sleep there hides his heavy head,
> And empty dreams on ev'ry leaf are spread.

Blake has used this image in other poems:

> Once a dream did weave a shade
> O'er my Angel-guarded bed. . . .

and

> Sweet dreams, form a shade
> O'er my lovely infant's head. . . .

suggest those dreams hidden under the leaves of the Tree of Sleep. Blake may have had his doubts about Darwin's elm; but to leave us none, he has illustrated his poem with an elm of the kind he must have seen often in his rambles in the country round London. Only the great trunk is shown—*ingens*, as Virgil says; but the heavily grained bark and the slender twigs growing [37] out of the trunk are characteristic of those pollarded elms that were until recently such beautiful features of the country outside London.

Lyca fears that her mother will not wish her to sleep; but when we realize what sleep it is that she has invoked, under the branches of the Elm of Hades, we can understand Lyca's dwelling upon the reluctance, otherwise incomprehensible, of her mother to allow her to sleep. What is more, she says that unless her mother sleeps, she herself cannot carry out her wish:

> "How can Lyca sleep
> If her mother weep?

> If her heart does ake
> Then let Lyca wake;
> If my mother sleep,
> Lyca shall not weep."

These words, taken as descriptive of any conceivable human situation, must seem trivial, if not meaningless; but if here we consider our myth, they take on meaning and precision; for Ceres, according to Taylor, is intellect, the divine consciousness, or higher self, which opposes the desire for oblivion that overcomes the "moist soul." Such a mother will not wish her daughter-soul to descend into the gloomy house of matter. But the soul so irresistibly attracted down is willing, indeed eager, for the "mother" to sleep, and all that belongs to immortality in her nature to become unconscious; for she is no passive victim. Her invocation of the powers of darkness, night, and the moon have the incantatory power of a spell of Hecate:

> "Frowning, frowning night,
> O'er this desart bright
> Let thy moon arise
> While I close my eyes."

We remember that according to Porphyry souls "descend" through the moon-governed Tropic of Cancer and, according to Plato, at midnight. There (so Taylor tells us) they drink a draught of Lethe from "the starry cup placed between Cancer and the Lion"; "hence oblivion, the companion of intoxication, there begins silently to creep into the recesses of the soul." And "when they arrive at the Lion" the empire of Pluto (who is material nature) begins, and the descending soul enters upon its new condition, in the caves or dens of the underworld. So Lyca leaves the country of everlasting summer for the caves of the underworld and remains, throughout the poems that follow, asleep.

We may see in the mourning of the little girl's father and mother, and in the loosing of her "slender dress" by the lioness who carries her into the caves, the pathos of mortal life as expressed by the figures on the Portland Vase. Lyca's weeping parents are the man and woman who sadly watch the death of their daughter; but although Blake may mean us to pause for a moment at this natural meaning of the symbol, we are swept on deeper into the mysteries; for who is the lion who encounters Lyca where she has lain down to sleep?

He is the lion of the Zodiac; Lyca has "arrived at the lion" and left the world of immortal spirits to enter Pluto's kingdom

> . . . the lion old
> Bow'd his mane of gold. . . .
>
> While the lioness
> Loos'd her slender dress,
> And naked they convey'd
> To caves the sleeping maid.

But what of the lioness? There is no lioness in the Zodiac; has Blake been carried away by his "vision"? In saying that the lioness too is a canonical symbol I hope that the illusions destroyed will be more than compensated by the realization of the extent of Blake's learning in the symbolic tradition and his imaginative mastery of his symbols. Taylor on the first page of his *Dissertation on the Mysteries* refers to an earlier work, *The Divine Legation of Moses* by Bishop Warburton; and to that work Blake must have turned; for there we learn that in the cave temples of Mithras (and Blake knew something of these also from Bryant) the priest and priestess who initiated adepts into the mysteries of the Cave were called the Lion and the Lioness. Lyca, too, is found by the Lion on "hallow'd ground"—the entrance to that same cave temple symbolizing the world; and there is a suggestion of a religious rite in the solemnity of the lines that tell the story.

In the text of the poem Lyca is described as a child seven years old, but in the plates she is shown as a grown woman; for the
35] attraction into generation involves sexuality. In the first plate she is shown with her lover, listening to the "wild birds' song" that led her astray. It is only by piecing together fragments of symbols to which Blake has returned in several contexts, in each adding something to his theme, that we arrive at the full meaning of many phrases which, taken alone, might seem accidental; but in Blake there is nothing accidental: Lyca has heard the voice of the "lureing bird of Eden," who elsewhere is called Leutha, or sexuality. That is why she is shown with a lover; Vala and her lover are shown under a similar tree full of birds, and in illustrat-
29] ing the Bible Blake has shown Eve naming the birds, a theme of which there is no mention in Genesis. Eve's birds are the lureing-birds of love. Lyca is married; for "souls proceeding into generation are the nymphs called Naiades," and these are called "married, as being conjoined to generation."

In another plate we see Lyca surrounded by her children, playing happily in the lion's den. But before the soul's descent, as Taylor says, "its energies are in their infantine state," as was Lyca in her "southern clime"—another theme that Blake was to take up in more than one later myth.

The most famous episode of the story Milton has used,

> . . . Proserpin gathering flours,
> Herself a fairer Floure by gloomy Dis
> Was gather'd, which cost Ceres all that pain
> To seek her through the world. . . .

Of this there is no mention in the story of Lyca; but Blake never
38] wasted anything; another maiden, Oothoon, in *Visions of the*

Daughters of Albion, is ravished, after gathering the flower of Leutha's vale, by Bromion, who carries her over the sea and imprisons her in a cave, where she remains lamenting. In the Greek myth the fatal flower was a hundred-headed golden narcissus; and the Marygold of Blake's poem has the same attribute of multiplicity, characteristic of the world of generation; for the flower says to the virgin,

> "Pluck thou my flower, Oothoon the mild!
> Another flower shall spring, because the soul of sweet delight
> Can never pass away."

Plotinus compares bodily life to "a beautiful but transient flower"; into this plant-like condition Narcissus was changed, the boy who fell in love with his reflection in the water, his physical body. Therefore, says Taylor, "Proserpina, . . . at the very instant of her descent into matter, is, with the utmost propriety, represented as eagerly engaged in plucking this fatal flower. . . ."

In his three early figures of the soul, Thel, Lyca, and Oothoon, Blake was not merely repeating himself; each represents a different possibility. Thel, a "dry soul," refuses to make the descent; is she wise? Blake was not quite sure, and returned to the theme in *Vala*. Lyca descends by a blind compulsion that is at the same time her destiny, and in the cave, though asleep, she is safe; but was her descent really a good one? Again Blake had after-thoughts when he returned to the figure of aged Earth, "her locks cover'd with grey despair," who so bitterly complains of her prison-house. Oothoon is the noblest, for in the Cave she does not forget her eternal nature. She is imprisoned in the watery [39] envelope of the body—the strange image of a woman fettered within a wave signifies this condition—and to be so fettered and yet awake is inevitably to suffer. Oothoon never ceases, in the world-cave, to proclaim the values of eternity, and to try to live by them. Blake in describing her was probably thinking of his friend Mary Wollstonecraft, who, like her son-in-law Shelley, refused to recognize any morality external to the soul; and there are phrases in Oothoon's speeches that recall also another woman whom Blake greatly admired and continually quoted, St. Teresa of Avila; for what are the saints but souls who live in time by the values of eternity?

Taylor follows Plotinus in giving a reason for the descent of souls which we have not yet found in Blake's treatment of the theme; soul descends, Plotinus says, in order that intellect—the higher divine principle—may follow, and so shine into the dark world of formless matter where, but for this descent, "nothing but irrational and brutal life" would be found. This life is, in Blake's poems, symbolized by the animals playing round Lyca in the lion's kingdom.

> Leopards, tygers, play
> Round her as she lay. . . .

These do not harm her; on the contrary, her coming appears to fill them with joy. In the old legend it is said that on the night of the marriage of Persephone to the King of Hades all the souls of the dead rejoiced, and Charon the ferryman rowed his empty boat on the river Lethe, singing—a theme that foreshadows the Christian myth of the Harrowing of Hell. In terms of the Eleusinian symbols, then, Demeter is intellect, Persephone the vital soul; and where the daughter goes, the mother must follow. Blake's poems follow faithfully the story of the wanderings of the mourning mother; for although he mentions two parents the father plays no active part:

> Rising from unrest,
> The trembling woman prest
> With feet of weary woe:
> She could no further go.

After wanderings that last for the symbolic seven days of the myth, the parents in their turn arrive at the lion:

> "Follow me," he said;
> "Weep not for the maid;
> In my palace deep
> Lyca lies asleep."

Unlike their mortal daughter, the immortal parents perceive his divine nature; he reveals himself as "A spirit arm'd in gold."

> On his head a crown,
> From his shoulders down
> Flow'd his golden hair.
> Gone was all their care.

This epiphany is the meaning of the mystery, the solution of the paradox of "above" and "below" towards which Blake was already moving. As the Alchemical text says, "That which is above is like that which is beneath, and that which is beneath is like that which is above, to perform the miracle of one thing." The king of the underworld is also divine; there is only one God, above or below. The parents remain with their child during her mortal existence, so fulfilling the necessity that divine intellect should be introduced into the world of matter.

> To this day they dwell
> In a lonely dell;
> Nor fear the wolvish howl
> Nor the lions' growl.

The lower natures of the Cave are not to be feared by the soul or by her still more divine parents.

"The Little Girl Lost" and "Found" must have been among the

last of *Songs of Innocence* to be written; and it seems possible that the idea from which arose *Songs of Experience* as a whole was the neo-Platonic theme which had captured Blake's imagination, the condition of the soul who "descends." The world of Experience is the Hades of souls lapsed from eternity; and each poem tells of some aspect of that condition, which to Blake seemed so terrible. Not only did he transfer these two poems to the new series; he also wrote an "Introduction," expanding the theme of Earth's sleep and awakening that prefaces "The Little Girl Lost." In this series we find many phrases taken from Plotinus' tractates *On the Nature and Origin of Evil* and *On the Descent of the Soul*, published in the year the poem was written—1794. Not only have we the "night," the "dew" of moisture, the soul made prisoner in a den on a "wat'ry shore," familiar images of neo-Platonism; "the lapse of the soul," according to Plotinus, "is to descend into matter, which renders her light, itself vigorous and pure, polluted and feeble." Blake uses Plotinus' terms; he tells of "The Holy Word" (The Divine Logos):

> Calling the lapsed Soul,
> And weeping in the evening dew;
> That might controll
> The starry pole,
> And fallen, fallen light renew!

The soul comes from beyond "the starry pole" (the northern gate) and need not be subject to the Zodiac under whose sway she lies bound. Plotinus writes that "the death of the soul is to descend into matter and to be filled with its darkness and deformity ... till after proper purgation it rises to things superior, and elevates its eye from the sordid mass; for, indeed, to descend into Hades and fall asleep in its dreary regions means nothing more than to be profoundly merged in the filth and obscurity of the body"; and Blake condenses "the sordid mass" and the ensuing sleep in a fine phrase "the slumberous mass":

> "O Earth, O Earth, return!
> Arise from out the dewy grass;
> Night is worn,
> And the morn
> Rises from the slumberous mass."

The soul of the world who as Lyca fell asleep, must now break her fetters, leave her watery prison in the cave-den, and return to her native country; and in "Earth's Answer" her exclamation

> "Break this heavy chain
> That does freeze my bones around"

might be a paraphrase of Plotinus' account of the condition of the lapsed soul: "She is reported also to be buried, and to be concealed in a cave; but when she converts herself to intelligence, then she breaks her fetters and ascends on high." In Plotinus' tractate Blake must have found confirmation of his own philosophy of Experience:

> Souls are able to rise from hence, carrying back with them an experience of what they have known and suffered in their fallen state; from whence they will learn how blessed it is to abide in the intelligible world.

But in these later poems we no longer have the lion-king; instead

> "Prison'd on watr'y shore,
> Starry Jealousy does keep my den:"

an early foreshadowing of Blake's Urizen, the moral tyrant of the

Prophetic Books, whose religion and laws prevail in the world that has forgotten eternity. In *The Marriage of Heaven and Hell* Blake protested against an error found in "All Bibles or sacred codes"—and he must have included Platonism—that there are two "existing principles" and that evil is "alone from the Body." His *Marriage of Heaven and Hell* proclaims this harmony of opposites, "as above, so below"—the philosophy of Alchemy. In Blake's ever-branching mythology, Urizen's consort, Ahania, continues the theme of fallen Earth. Ahania, the Earth, outcast of the "Bibles or sacred codes," is in truth the consort of heaven. Earth's protest to the "selfish father of men,"

> "Cruel, jealous, selfish fear!
> Can delight,
> Chain'd in night,
> The virgins of youth and morning bear?"

is taken up by Ahania:

> "But now alone over rocks, mountains,
> Cast out from thy lovely bosom,
> Cruel jealousy! selfish fear!
> Self-destroying, how can delight
> Renew in these chains of darkness,
> Where bones of beasts are strown
> On bleak and snowy mountains,
> Where bones from the birth are buried
> Before they see the light?"

There is a plate showing Ahania in her virgin-form; but she is typically the Ceres figure, fruitful mother earth. She is called the "furrow'd field," and "thou corn field ... thou vegetater happy"; but Urizen disowns her, calling her a "death-shadow" (since earth is the shadow of heaven) and "mother of

Pestilence," because she draws the souls down into generation. She pleads with Urizen to remember and restore the due harmony when Earth's "virgins of youth and morning" were not disowned by heaven:

> "When he gave my happy soul
> To the sons of eternal joy,
> When he took the daughters of life
> Into my chambers of love,
> When I found babes of bliss on my beds. . . ."

and "eternal births sung round Ahania." Without the harmony of heaven and earth, Ahania bitterly mourns that the grave may "mock & laugh at the plow'd field, saying 'I am the nourisher, thou the destroyer'"—for birth is, as the Greek philosophers taught, a death, and death an escape from the horror of mortality.

The due relation of heaven and earth is not merely a contrast of life and death; it is rather that of sower and sown. In the restoration of all things starry Urizen will once more be the husband and husbandman of Earth; and in the Ninth Night of *The Four Zoas* Blake returned for the last time to the myth of the two goddesses. We find Ahania's story strangely beginning where we might rather expect it to end, with her death and burial:

> . . . she fell down dead at the feet of Urizen
> Outstretch'd, a smiling corse: they buried her in a silent cave.

—a brief summary of the story of Persephone, Lyca, and all souls who descend. Next, the earth is plowed by Urizen and his sons; and then, in an image that recalls the Platonic comparison of souls to stars, it is sown by Urizen

> . . . his skirt fill'd with immortal souls.
> Howling & Wailing fly the souls from Urizen's strong hand,
> For from the hand of Urizen the myriads fall like stars
> Into their own appointed places. . . .

No longer "Starry Jealousy," Urizen is still the sower of stars. The human harvest begins to grow on earth, "& in silent fear they look out from their graves"; at last Urizen and his sons

> Reap'd the wide Universe & bound in sheaves a wondrous
>   harvest.

40] A plate in *Milton* shows Ahania with a man and woman ripening as the corn of earth.

Ahania's final apotheosis brings us back once more to the seasonal descent and resurrection of Persephone in an image that beautifully combines the natural and the higher meanings of the symbol; Ahania, like Persephone, is to descend and return, "a Self-renewing Vision":

> "The spring, the summer, to be thine; then sleep the wintry
>   days
> In silken garments spun by her own hands against her
>   funeral"

—on those looms of the Cave where mortal garments are woven:

> "The winter thou shalt plow & lay thy stores into thy barns
> Expecting to receive Ahania in the spring with joy."

There is no mistaking the old story; and, again, there is an unbroken continuity from the first appearance of the promise that Earth

> Shall arise and seek
> For her maker meek

to the perfected mystery of Christian theology.

In her apotheosis Ahania emerges as the great goddess Ceres, or Juno, who by bathing renews her virginity; or as the even more highly exalted Christian figure of the Blessed Virgin, whose Assumption is Catholic doctrine.

> And Lo, like the harvest Moon, Ahania cast off her death clothes;
> She folded them up in care, in silence, & her bright'ning limbs
> Bath'd in the clear spring of the rock; then from her dark-some cave
> Issu'd in majesty divine. . . .
> And bright Ahania took her seat by Urizen in songs & joy.

[41]   A plate in Bryant's *Mythology* expresses, in the form of an emblem, the mystery of the earth-goddess; in her hand she holds the seed of poppies, the flowers of sleep, and the seed of corn, emblem of resurrection; for the earth is the place of the soul's sleep and waking, death and resurrection; in the words of St. Paul, "It is sown in corruption; it is raised in incorruption. . . . It is sown a natural body; it is raised a spiritual body." And as Blake placed at the beginning of *Songs of Experience* an emblem of the death of the soul, and two poems telling of her burial in the cave or grave of earth, so he added a last plate on which he inscribed the words "It is Raised a Spiritual Body" upon an apostolic figure who baptizes a soul bound into a mor-
[42] tal body by two weeping females. The poem "To Tirzah" and its emblem expresses Blake's Christian resolution of the paradox of death-in-life which so long continued to trouble him; once more, he has deepened and baptized the ancient theme of the mystery of the corn.

Whate'er is Born of Mortal Birth
Must be consumed with the Earth
To rise from Generation free:
Then what have I to do with thee?

The Sexes sprung from Shame & Pride,
Blow'd in the morn; in evening died;
But Mercy chang'd Death into Sleep;
The Sexes rose to work & weep.

Thou, Mother of my Mortal part,
With cruelty didst mould my Heart,
And with false self-decieving tears
Didst bind my Nostrils, Eyes, & Ears:

Didst close my Tongue in senseless clay,
And me to Mortal Life betray.
The Death of Jesus set me free:
Then what have I to do with thee?

THE MYTH OF THE GREAT YEAR

Blake returned again and again to the problem of evil in the symbolic terms of a "descent" of the soul from a world of spiritual light into a world of material darkness; but behind the story of the soul lies the cosmic problem of the origin and nature of the world. The original "descent" of light, or spirit, into matter, or darkness, has been expressed in many fables: the dismembering of Osiris and the scattering of his body over the earth; the laceration of Dionysus; the *deus absconditus*, or hidden god, of Alchemy, made prisoner in matter. As the individual soul has its cycle of descent and return, so have these symbolic figures of the divine power in the cosmos itself.

Blake, who considered Paracelsus as great as Shakespeare, knew the Alchemical tradition; and that strange poem "The Crystal Cabinet" seems to summarize the Alchemical doctrine of the imprisoning of light in matter. The very title is Alchemical; the "cabinet" is a term used by Thomas Vaughan (Eugenius Philatethes), brother of the poet Henry Vaughan, for the physical body in which spirit dwells. In his book *Aula Lucis* (the tent of light) he writes that "matter is the house of light . . . when he (that is light or spirit) first enters it, it is a glorious transparent room, a crystal castle, and he lives like a Familiar in diamonds. He hath the liberty to look out at the windows, his love is all in his sight: I mean that liquid Venus which lures him in; but this continues not long," says Vaughan; for the feminine watery principle makes the light her prisoner, so that at last "he is quite shut up in darkness." The same story is told in Blake's poem:

> The Maiden caught me in the Wild
> Where I was dancing merrily;
> She put me into her Cabinet
> And Lock'd me up with a golden Key.

The maiden is our by now familiar water-nymph or "liquid Venus," and the merry dancer the light or spirit which she captures and encloses in a body. In Blake's poem, too, the prisoner can at first look out of the windows, but is at last snared in a threefold prison (another Alchemical detail of the process) and generated as

> A weeping Babe upon the wild. . . .

The ensnaring of spirit in matter is more fully embodied in another fragment of myth, written, according to Margoliouth (who made a study of the *Vala* manuscript), earlier than the first draft of the poem *Vala*. This fragment was added to the poem when it was finally revised and called *The Four Zoas*; and it remains, in Night the First, like an outcrop of older rock. Tharmas is the animating spirit who becomes entangled and ensnared by the feminine "wat'ry" principle, Enion; he is the Alchemical *deus absconditus*, captured and imprisoned. The source of all subsequent Alchemical versions of this myth was known to Blake, for in *The Song of Los*, written in 1792, he mentions Hermes

Trismegistus; and it is evident that he had read the *Hermetica*, no doubt in Everard's seventeenth-century translation, *The Divine Pymander of Hermes Trismegistus*. Berkeley or Milton may first have led Blake to read this work; or perhaps Vaughan, who also constantly quotes him. *Aula Lucis* is based upon the same allegory in the second Book of the *Hermetica* that Blake has used in the myth of Enion and Tharmas; and Blake seems to have known both versions.

First of all things, the Pymander says, there was light; but from the eye of the light itself there arose a moist cloud of darkness, feminine, heavy, and, as the myth says, inexpressibly sorrowful. From the mingling of the light with this moist cloud, the elements and the whole universe of nature are produced. Paracelsus knew this myth; for his "Great Mystery," Nature, he describes as cloud, or smoke, and all her creatures, according to Paracelsus, "shall pass away and vanish into nothing but smoke, they shall all end in a fume." Blake too calls the physical body a "cloud"; and the Hermetic and Paracelsian Great Mystery reappears as Blake's "Shadowy Female," Vala, who, as Nature, is often called the "Mystery" and likened to a cloud, and to smoke.

Next there follows the ensnaring of man in nature; for man as he is at first created is a spiritual being, but then (so the Hermetic myth continues) he stoops and looks down through the planetary spheres, and far below he catches sight (like Narcissus in another version of the same story) of his image reflected in the water; with this image he falls in love; the soul, in other words, identifies itself with the body. The moist feminine principle thereupon wraps herself about him, and man becomes her prisoner. This episode Blake has told in the story of Tharmas:

> . . . bending from his Clouds, he stoop'd his innocent head,
> And stretching out his holy hand in the vast deep sublime,
> [43]   Turn'd round the circle of Destiny with tears & bitter sighs
> And said: "Return, O wanderer, when the day of Clouds is o'er."

> So saying, he sunk down, & flow'd among her filmy Woof,. . . .
> In gnawing pain drawn out by her lov'd fingers, every nerve
> She counted, every vein & lacteal, threading them among
> Her woof of terror.

From this ensnaring of an immortal spirit in a mortal body there is produced a Spectre of double nature, generated man, who is, like the ancient Gilgamesh, part immortal, part mortal; Blake attempted to symbolize this condition as a hermaphrodite, later dropped from the myth. The name of this figure— Tharmas—seems to derive from the Greek word *thaumas* (wonder), used to describe the image of man reflected in the water, "a wonder most wonderful," as the Pymander says. The terrible water-garment (another passage in the *Hermetica* describes the bodily garment as "the web of Ignorance, the bond of Corruption, the dark Coverture, the living Death, the sensible Carcasse, the Sepulchre, carried about with us") is retained in Blake's later representations of fallen man, sunk in deadly sleep [44] on a rock sunk in the ocean, his body enwoven and its fibres drawn out and threaded, like Tharmas, into a "woof of terror."

There are many details that relate the early Spectre of Tharmas to Alchemical and Hermetic sources; but by the time he began writing the surviving version of *Vala* Blake had abandoned this figure; and when Tharmas reappears in Night the Third, it is a far more grandly imagined god who speaks from the Paracelsian "smoke" in which he has become involved:

> . . . one like a shadow of smoke appear'd,
> And human bones rattling together in the smoke & stamping
> The nether Abyss, & gnashing in fierce despair, . . .
> Struggling to utter the voice of Man, struggling to take the
>   features of Man, struggling
> To take the limbs of Man, at length emerging from the smoke
> Of Urizen dashed in pieces from his precipitant fall,

> Tharmas rear'd up his hands & stood on the affrighted
> Ocean. . . .

This tragic figure resembles none of the sea-gods, Oceanus, Phorcys, or Poseidon; for none of these express suffering. He speaks as the dismembered god dissolved in the flux of matter who seeks to reassume his human form:

> "My skull riven into filaments, my eyes into sea jellies
> Floating upon the tide wander bubbling & bubbling,
> Uttering my lamentations & begetting little monsters. . . .
> In all my rivers. . . .

Tharmas' dead and scattered bones are taken from a Biblical image, in which Blake found yet another version of the dismembering and resurrection of the spirit; in Ezekiel's Valley of Dry Bones he saw a parallel with Osiris' scattered members:

> And he said unto me, Son of man, can these bones live? . . .
> Thus saith the Lord God unto these bones; Behold, I will cause
> breath to enter into you, and ye shall live. . . . and as I proph-
> esied, there was a noise, and behold a shaking, and the bones
> came together, bone to his bone.

This is the image that Blake has so dramatically humanized—to use his own word.

Bryant, in his all-permissive *Mythology*, identifies "Thaumas, Thamas, or Thamuz" with Dionysus. Because Blake made such extensive use of the first part of Taylor's *Dissertation on the Mysteries* it would have been very strange if he had not used this pretext to add to the story of the Hermetic Thaumas that of the Orphic Dionysus, in the story of whose "fall into Division & his Resurrection to Unity" he found yet another version of the ensnaring of spirit in matter. The myth of Dionysus, or Bacchus, as given by

Taylor, tells how the god, while still a child, is betrayed through the hostility of Juno, who sends the Titans to offer him playthings. One of these is a looking-glass. The child-god becomes fascinated by his reflection; and while he is gazing into the glass the Titans tear him to pieces, then first boil his members, and afterwards roast them. At this point Zeus intervenes and hurls his thunder at the Titans, giving the body of the god to be properly interred by Apollo. But his heart has been snatched away by Pallas and preserved; and from this living heart he is regenerated.

Taylor explains the symbols; before the "descent" of the god, there must be an image established in matter; as in the Hermetic myth the archetypal man identifies himself with, and so enters, the "unreasonable image" or reflection, the body, so does Dionysus identify himself with his reflection. He is thereupon "distributed," as Taylor says, in matter; the "boiling" and "roasting" of the god is symbolic of the descent into matter (water) and the reascent of the spirit through fire. Blake's Tharmas, like Dionysus, is constantly described as lacerated, scattered, and distributed in the ocean, striving to reascend through the "smoke" into his former spiritual condition.

All these myths of captivation by a mirror, or a reflection in water, have the same meaning; and the symbolism persisted in the Alchemical tradition from which Jakob Boehme, whom Blake so greatly revered, must have derived his "Glass of the Abyss"; for the traditional language of symbols, seemingly protean, leads us back, again and again, to the same themes. There is, says Boehme, "a Glass in the Abyss, in which the source beholds itself." In Boehme also this Glass is a feminine principle, "a Virgin of the temple, wherein the wrathfulness of the flesh discerns itself infinitely without number"; and we may remember that mermaids long continued to lure sailors to their death in the sea by the magic of the looking-glass they carried in their hands.

We must now leave the myth of Tharmas and Enion and

examine that strange poem "The Mental Traveller." This poem tells of an infant boy, sacrificed by "a Woman Old." But then the boy-victim grows older and the woman younger, until he obtains the mastery, and binds her down; the process continues and the boy babe becomes an old man, the woman old a female infant; then comes a reversal, the female growing older and the male younger, until the poem ends with the return of the male babe, about to be sacrificed by a woman old—a completed cycle.

In the first edition of *A Vision* William Butler Yeats referred to Blake's poem as a key to his own thought; he admits that he had not understood the poem, when, over thirty years earlier, he had collaborated with Edwin J. Ellis in a big book on the philosophy of William Blake. "We had understood the details," he wrote, "but not the poem as a whole, nor the myth, the perpetual return to the same thing; nor that which certainly moved Blake to write it." He then goes on to say that it is to be understood by the "double cones" of his own *A Vision*, and concludes, "the woman and the man are two conflicting gyres growing at one another's expense."

[45]

Yeats's *A Vision* is based on the continual sequence of phases throughout history, symbolized by a continual movement between two cones, the apex of one touching the base of the other; and Yeats understood that Blake's poem also is on the theme of historical cycles. Like Blake, he chooses to mystify us, attributing his own symbolism, as Blake often does, to spiritual "instructors"; yet it is quite plain that he had now discovered Blake's source, and with it a theme that moved him deeply enough to inspire his own *A Vision*, besides many poems. The source is in fact Plato, whose *Politicus* appeared for the first time in English, in Taylor's translation, in 1804, the year in which Blake probably wrote "A Mental Traveller." Here we find the meaning of the gyres—Blake's as well as Yeats's. Plato also sees history as a perpetual movement between two poles; sometimes God conducts the universe, and controls its revolutions; at another time He leaves it to its own devices. Plato uses the simile of a spring tightly wound in one direction for a certain time, and unwinding itself spontaneously when it is released, until it has run down; thus the world, when it is no longer conducted by the god, "proceeds by itself, and, being thus left for a time, performs many myriads of retrograde revolutions." This is the Great Year of the ancient world; for behind the Greek myth lie Babylonian and Indian myths still more ancient. Plato's image of the coiled spring gave Yeats, directly or indirectly, his gyres.

But why was Yeats so certain that Blake's two figures, with their alternations of youth and age, correspond to the Platonic cycles? At those times, Plato says, when the divine ruler leaves the earth to revolve in retrograde, man advances, as now, from youth to age; but when the god is in control, man progresses from age to youth. The literalness of Plato's imagery is no less striking than that of Blake's poem:

> ... The white hairs of those more advanced in years then become black, and the cheeks of those that had beards become smooth; and thus each was restored to the past flower of his age. The bodies, likewise, of such as were in the bloom of youth, becoming smoother and smaller every day and night, again returning to the nature of a child recently born. . . . And at length their bodies rapidly wasting away, perished.

Thus man enters Saturn's golden country, "as a little child."

The Marriage of Heaven and Hell begins with the pronouncement [46] that a new age is begun—the New Age that Swedenborg declared had begun in 1757—and we see in the accompanying designs, first, a woman in labour giving birth to a child; then the flaming babe, Orc, spirit of revolution; and in "A Song of Liberty" the triumph of this new Messiah over the aged Urizen is foretold. But in "The Mental Traveller" the child is both an initial

and a terminal state; the Golden Age is not only the beginning
from which we come, but the end to which we strive:

> For there the Babe is born in joy
> That was begotten in dire woe;
> Just as we Reap in joy the fruit
> Which we in bitter tears did sow.

No sooner is the Babe born than he is sacrificed:

> And if the Babe is born a Boy
> He's given to a Woman Old,
> Who nails him down upon a rock,
> Catches his shrieks in cups of gold.
>
> She binds iron thorns around his head,
> She pierces both his hands & feet,
> She cuts the heart out at his side
> To make him feel both cold & heat.

[47]

The Babe is manacled to a rock like Prometheus; he wears
Christ's crown of thorns; and his heart is cut out by "a Woman
Old," as Dionysus was lacerated by Juno. The parallel between
Christ and Dionysus, both sacrificed, both associated with the
symbolism of the vine, has often been observed; and have we
not in the breaking of the sacramental bread another parallel to
the dismemberment of those older gods whose bodies were
scattered over the earth? Yeats too brought together the myths of
Christ and Dionysus in his play *The Resurrection*: The Resurrection
of Christ is the beginning of a New Age; and Yeats describes the
beginning of the new gyre under the old symbol. The goddess
Pallas saves the living heart from which the god is reborn:

> I saw a staring virgin stand
> Where holy Dionysus died,
> And tear the heart out of his side,

And lay the heart upon her hand
And bear that beating heart away;
And then did all the Muses sing
Of Magnus Annus at the spring,
As though God's death were but a play.

In Yeat's poem, as in Blake's, the incarnation and sacrifice of the god symbolizes the divine influx into history which initiates a new revolution of the Great Year.

But why should Blake and Yeats both have supposed the sacrifice of Dionysus to be symbolically associated with Plato's Great Year? This belongs to the Orphic tradition, known to both poets through, again, Thomas Taylor's *Dissertation*, a work that Yeats knew and admired as well as Blake. Dionysus is a god of two aspects, child and man; he is sometimes depicted as a bearded [48] man holding on his knees his own *alter ego*; and it is the child who is the more powerful. This Taylor explains:

> . . . by the puerile state of Bacchus at the period of his laceration, the flourishing condition of an intellectual nature is implied; since, according to the Orphic theology, souls, while under the government of Saturn, who is pure intellect, instead of proceeding, as now, from youth to age, advance in retrograde progression from age to youth.

Distributed into the material world, the spiritual principle ages and weakens, under the power of the opposing principle, feminine and material, of the body; for Blake's man and woman are spirit and matter, or, on another level, soul and body. Sallust says that "when the body with which a soul is connected is beautiful and young, then the soul is oppressed and its vigour diminished; but when this grows old, the soul revives, and increases in strength and vigour." This is a key to the real meaning of Plato's fable: the principle that grows from age to youth is not body but soul, or intellect, waxing as body wanes.

There is every reason, then, for Blake to have made the sacrifice of the child-god stand at the beginning of the Great Year. There is plenty of traditional precedent, also, for placing the Incarnation of Jesus at the beginning of such a cycle. Blake no doubt knew Virgil's legendary prophecy of a new golden age taken throughout the Middle Ages to refer to the birth of Christ:

> The last great age, foretold by sacred rhymes,
> Renews its finished course: Saturnian times
> Roll round again; and mighty years, begun
> From their first orb, in radiant circles run.
> The base degenerate iron offspring ends:
> The golden progeny from heaven descends.

This is why Yeats also places at the beginning of his play on the theme of Christ an allusion to the sacrifice of Dionysus, and the beginning of the Great Year. In Yeats's play the beating heart of Dionysus animates the risen Christ; and it is, significantly, a Greek who presses his hand to the side of Christ and cries "The heart of a phantom is beating!"—a phantom being, like Blake's Spectre, in terms of the Platonic symbolism, a material body; and Thomas, seeking conviction of the reality of the Resurrection, puts "his hand where the heart is."

To return to Blake's poem: the "Woman Old" (who is also, of course, Juno) we may identify with the watery Enion, who counted every nerve, "every vein and lacteal," of Tharmas, and threaded "them among Her woof of terror"; for

> Her fingers number every Nerve,
> Just as a Miser counts his gold;
> She lives upon his shrieks & cries,
> And she grows young as he grows old.

Blake, perhaps to bring his own myth into conformity with the laceration of Dionysus, added a passage to *The Four Zoas* which introduces the image of the lacerated infant; Tharmas asks Enion,

> Why wilt thou Examine every little fibre of my soul,
> Spreading them out before the sun like stalks of flax to dry?
> The infant joy is beautiful, but its anatomy
> Horrible, Ghast & Deadly. . . .

The poem "To Tirzah," addressed to the cruel "Mother of my Mortal part," also specifies the *heart* that she sacrifices; and the sacrifice of Albion by Rahab and Tirzah is a later development of the same theme.

[49]

In Plato's myth, the world is alternately conducted, and abandoned, by the god; there is only one agent. When the world is no longer guided by Saturn, "it proceeds by itself, and being thus left for a time, performs many myriads of retrograde revolutions"; but Blake's female is in accordance with a whole body of tradition which symbolizes matter as a feminine principle. As the initial male spiritual impulse weakens into old age, the feminine principle grows towards her prime; but this process passes through many phases. The male Babe grows in strength

> Till he becomes a bleeding youth
> And she becomes a Virgin bright;
> Then he rends up his Manacles
> And binds her down for his delight.

This story is told at greater length in the myth of Orc, who also, Prometheus-like, rends his manacles at the beginning of Blake's New Age, "on the Canadian wilds," to master the "Shadowy female," Nature. There follows a period of harmony between spirit and matter; an age of great art, perhaps, when matter is moulded by imagination and takes the imprint of spirit. Blake does not, in "The Mental Traveller," specify particular historical periods; but elsewhere he describes the phases of history in terms of twenty-seven "Churches"—a piece of symbolism taken from Swedenborg. These "Churches" succeed one another from Adam to the end of the "six thousand years" of time; we find them again in Yeats's twenty-eight phases of the moon. Boehme also wrote of seven "times" between Adam and the end of the world, each with its different character, and he too influenced Blake's thought upon the phases of history. But in "The Mental Traveller" Blake's concern is the underlying process, and not the characteristics of each phase.

An equilibrium between spirit and matter is inevitably succeeded by decadence, since nothing ever remains the same. "Things thought too long can be no longer thought," Yeats wrote, in a phrase that summarizes the essential meaning of Blake's poem. There succeeds a period, no longer of creation, but of the enjoyment of the accumulated treasures of civilization,

> Which he by industry had got.
> And these are the gems of the Human Soul,
> The rubies & pearls of a lovesick eye,
> The countless gold of the akeing heart,
> The martyr's groan & the lover's sigh.

The "industry" of the spirit is the love and suffering of martyrs and lovers; the record of these remains in works of art and poetry, as the treasures of mankind. Humankind are the "Guests," fed (for man does not live by bread alone) at the "house" of an ancient civilization. In the formative and potent years of civilization these treasures are in the making; in the decline, enjoyed and distributed:

> They are his meat, they are his drink;
> He feeds the Beggar & the Poor

And the wayfaring Traveller:
For ever open is his door.

Yeats (from his subsequent writings we may guess that it was he
and not Ellis) well understood this part of Blake's poem, when
he wrote in the 1893 commentary:

The wealth of his soul consists in the accumulation of his
own smiles and tears.... He is male, and mental, and
these things make the joy of others, whom he "teaches in
song"—as the overworked phrase has it—what he "learned in
suffering."

His grief is their eternal joy;
They make the roofs & walls to ring;
Till from the fire on the hearth
A little Female Babe does spring.

The creative impulse is now spent; and from its decadence a new
age has begun, the gyre is reversed, and a phase of materialism
commences. The spiritual impulse is exhausted:

He wanders weeping far away,
Untill some other take him in. . . .

Blake is still pursuing his historical allegory; for a spent culture
may be "taken in," to renew its energy in some young and vital
nation, as Greek culture was "taken in" by the Renaissance, the
Jewish tradition by Christianity, and possibly at the present time
the ancient East by the modern West.

Yeats must have pondered the theme of the gyres for many
years; for the closing lines of "The Resurrection" are a superb
restatement of Blake's meaning, and the best possible commen-
tary on the earlier poem:

> Everything that man esteems
> Endures a moment or a day.
> Love's pleasure drives his love away,
> The painter's brush consumes his dreams;
> The herald's cry, the soldier's tread
> Exhaust his glory and his might:
> Whatever flames upon the night
> Man's own resinous heart has fed.

Achievement in realization is, in both poems, an impulse of the spirit, spent; and again in Yeats's poem we find the image of the deathless heart of Dionysus, "resinous," like his emblem the fircone. Yeats's poem may be the finer rhetoric; but the imaginative foundations had been laid by Blake, and Yeats has but clarified and elaborated the thought and images of "The Mental Traveller."

But Blake has more to say; we return to his poem at the point of reversal. The god no longer guides the world; and at this moment, when aged and weary spirit embraces the infant female, Saturn's Golden Age ends, or, in Blake's image (which has the same symbolic meaning), the vision of eternity, or Eden, fades, as spirit embraces matter:

> And to allay his freezing Age
> The Poor Man takes her in his arms;
> The Cottage fades before his sight,
> The Garden & its lovely Charms.

The fading garden also occurs in the myth of Enion and Tharmas; it forebodes the Fall of Man. Tharmas says:

> . . . "O Vala, once I liv'd in a garden of delight;
> I waken'd Enion in the morning, & she turn'd away
> Among the apple trees; & all the garden of delight

Swam like a dream before my eyes. I went to seek the steps
Of Enion in the gardens, & the shadows compass'd me
And clos'd me in a wat'ry world of woe where Enion stood
Trembling before me like a shadow, like a mist, like air."

Blake, no less than Plato, saw the phase of material dominance as the iron-age of the world; and he describes its spiritual desolation in terms of the symbols he habitually associated with the philosophy of science, Newton's globes in space, and the desert of matter uninformed by spirit. When man lives imaginatively, his world is determined by quality; his world is what he experiences, and is therefore "flat," as it appears to the senses:

And on its verge the Sun rises & sets, the Clouds bow
To meet the flat Earth & the Sea in such an order'd Space:
The Starry heavens reach no further, but here bend and set
On all sides, & the two Poles turn on their valves of gold. . . .

This is the world of art; but the materialist builds his world in terms of quantity, and of scientific abstractions:

For the Eye altering alters all;
The Senses roll themselves in fear,
And the flat Earth becomes a Ball;

The stars, sun, Moon, all shrink away,
A desart vast without a bound,
And nothing left to eat or drink,
And a dark desart all around.

The Newtonian solar system of globes spinning in immeasurable space is not the world of human perception:

As to that false appearance which appears to the reasoner
As of a Globe rolling thro' Voidness, it is a delusion. . . .

Under the spell of Newtonian science man has confused his abstractions with his experiences. To the hypothetical "Atoms" and "Particles" of science Blake allows no substantial existence, for they are unknown to human experience; they are a "desart"; for for what is a desert but a vast expanse of particles where no life is? But seen with the eye of imagination nothing is merely quantitative:

> And every sand becomes a Gem
> Reflected in the beams divine;
> Blown back they blind the mocking Eye,
> But still in Israel's paths they shine.
>
> The Atoms of Democritus
> And Newton's Particles of light
> Are sands upon the Red sea shore,
> Where Israel's tents do shine so bright.

In a scientific phase, intellect is no longer engaged in the "binding" of imaginative form, in art; instead it "pursues" matter through the labyrinths of scientific research. Blake uses the word labyrinth, or maze, in the sense in which he found it used in a passage of Thomas Taylor, who wrote that "to pursue matter, through its infinite divisions, and wander in its dark labyrinths, is the employment of the philosophy in vogue"—that is, science:

> And on the desart wild they both
> Wander in terror & dismay.
>
> Like the wild Stag she flees away,
> Her fear plants many a thicket wild;
> While he pursues her night & day,
> By various arts of Love beguil'd,
> By various arts of Love & Hate,

Till the wide desart planted o'er
With Labyrinths of wayward Love. . . .

Again we find a parallel in the story of Enion and Tharmas; for
Enion begs Tharmas to build "mazes" and "labyrinths" for her.
In this wish he recognizes the onset of a phase of materialism
and turns the Circle of Destiny "with tears & bitter sighs"; for a
"day of Clouds" is dawning.

But the flowering of a period of science brings round, in its
turn, its antithesis. Perhaps we ourselves live at such a moment;
for has not the great age of materialist thought, from Descartes
to Einstein, come full circle round to a dematerialization of the
very concept of matter? The maiden weakens, and the youth
moves once more towards his prime. So Blake envisages New-
ton's globes "rolling thro' Voidness" giving place once more to
the imaginative vision; as the pursuit nears its end, and Eden
returns:

The Sun & Stars are nearer roll'd.

The trees bring forth sweet Extacy
To all who in the desart roam;
Till many a City there is Built,
And many a pleasant Shepherd's home.

Materialism becomes in its turn a spent force, whose task of
nourishing its opposite principle is accomplished. The new
Babe—Christ or Dionysus—enters history at the moment when,
in the completeness of achievement, the materialist dominance
is both at its height and at its limit:

But when they find the frowning Babe,
Terror strikes thro' the region wide:
They cry "The Babe! the Babe is Born!"
And flee away on Every side.

Yeats relates that cry to the beginning of the Christian era, which was for him, as for Blake, the overthrow of rational Rome by the forces higher than reason: "Meanwhile the irrational forces that would create confusion and uproar as with the cry 'The Babe! the Babe is Born'—the women speaking unknown tongues, the barbers and weavers expounding Divine revelation with all the vulgarity of their servitude. . . ." The barbers and weavers are a leaf Yeats has taken from Gibbon's *Decline and Fall of the Roman Empire*, a book Blake too had read; and much as he disliked Gibbon's anti-Christianity, he certainly saw the rise and fall of empire through his eyes.

The processes of human history, Blake finally indicates, are divinely directed; they can neither be arrested nor diverted. The Divine Child will descend when his time comes, and no human agent can turn aside the course of history,

> For who dare touch the frowning form,
> His arm is wither'd to its root

[50] like King Jeroboam, whose arm was paralyzed when he attempted to seize a man of God who had prophesied the birth of a new king who would pull down old altars; or like Uzzah, who was killed when he tried to stop the holy Ark in its progress. ". . . man is either the ark of God or a phantom of the earth & of the water," Blake wrote in the margin of Lavater's *Aphorisms*; "if thou seekest by human policy to guide this ark, remember Uzzah. . . ." And so with the Babe, whether the divine principle be "born in joy," as at the incarnation of Christ, or, as in the last epiphany, "frowning" for the Last Judgment of the world; for Blake suggests that event in an image from the Book of Revelation which tells how at the end the stars will fall from heaven "even as a fig tree casteth her untimely figs"—

And every Tree does shed its fruit.

51] Blake's "frowning Babe" was Orc, the spirit of revolution he welcomed alike in France and in America as the birth of a new phase in human history, and a new manifestation of the divine spirit, in its terrible aspect, judging and purging with fire. Is this to be the end of all things, or only of a world cycle? Yeats, a follower of Plato and the *Vedas*, we might expect to hold the ancient cyclic view of history (as did James Joyce, for whom history is "the same anew"). The strength of Plato's influence on Blake can be seen from the fact that, his Christianity notwithstanding, he also does so; for writing of the Swedenborgian Twenty-seven Churches he concludes,

And where Luther ends Adam begins again in Eternal Circle.

So at the end of "A Mental Traveller" the Woman Old again appears to sacrifice the child, and the cycle begins anew.

The smooth uninterrupted progression of Blake's unemphatic quatrains leads us round to the inevitable sacrifice with a sort of grave indifference. Yeats writes that to the Muses "God's death" is "but a play"; yet Blake's poem is playful, whereas Yeats, writing of the gyres, is deeply dismayed by that ever-turning circle, the end of the Christian era, and what seems an impending reversal:

Turning and turning in the widening gyre
The falcon cannot hear the falconer;
Things fall apart; the centre cannot hold;
Mere anarchy is loosed upon the world,
The blood-dimmed tide is loosed—

Antichrist approaches the place of Incarnation, in a form more terrible than Blake's frowning babe:

> And what rough beast, its hour come round at last
> Slouches towards Bethlehem to be born?

Blake saw in the New Age "the return of Adam into Paradise"—
as he tells in *The Marriage of Heaven and Hell*; Orc, the frowning babe,
though a rough beast, is holy. In 1801, perhaps in a hopeful
mood because of the peace with France then about to be con-
cluded, he wrote to his friend Flaxman, who shared Blake's
knowledge of the Swedenborgian system: "The Kingdoms of
this World are now become the Kingdoms of God & His Christ,
& we shall reign with him for ever and ever. The Reign of Litera-
ture & the Arts commences." Who can say that the poet who so
greatly embodied what he desired was mistaken?

THE NETHER-WORLD
OF ALCHEMY

Blake paid Socrates the compliment of calling him "a kind of brother," and allowed Plato the honour of having anticipated his own ideas on poetry and the arts; but of only two masters did he write with unqualified admiration, and these were Alchemists. In *The Marriage of Heaven and Hell* he says "Any man of mechanical talents" might from the writings of Paracelsus or Jakob Boehme "produce ten thousand volumes of equal value with Swedenborg's"; and in a verse letter to Flaxman he recalls his early masters: Isaiah and Ezra, Shakespeare and Milton, then

> Paracelsus & Behmen appear'd to me, terrors appear'd in the
>   Heavens above
> And in Hell beneath. . . .

From these passages we may gather that what fired Blake's imagination in the Alchemical philosophy was the teaching of the famous Smaragdine Table of Hermes Trismegistus (Blake names this work in *Jerusalem*): "That which is above is like that which is beneath, and that which is beneath is like that which is above, to work the miracles of one thing." *The Marriage of Heaven and Hell*, often said to contain Blake's most original thought, is in truth an impassioned re-statement of the philosophy of Alchemy.

From the enthusiasm of his praise we know that finally he was with the Alchemists and not with those neo-Platonists who see all that is "beneath" as evil. Plotinus urges the soul to fly to "our father's delightful land," as Thel does; but that was not Blake's answer, and in *The Book of Thel* we first find Blake presenting the philosophy of Alchemy as the solution of the problems of duality.

Thel herself may be named from the charming figure of [52] Thalia ("the blossoming one"), who in Thomas Vaughan's *Lumen de Lumine* initiates the Alchemist Eugenius Philalethes into the mysteries of "that which is beneath." Philalethes meets Thalia in a living "temple of nature," where the murmur of bees—the generating souls—may be heard; thence she leads him into the underworld, where she shows him an altar shaped as a cube (the traditional symbol of earth), where a young snake hatches from the roots of an old rotten tree. Still deeper is a cave, smelling of the grave; and this, Thalia tells her initiate, is the inmost sanctuary of Nature's mysteries, where death perpetually gives place to regeneration; as Thel was shown

> . . . the secrets of the land unknown.
> She saw the couches of the dead, & where the fibrous roots
> Of every heart on earth infixes deep its restless twists. . . .

The roots of life are in death.

Thel's motto summarizes the theme of the poem that bears her name, later expanded in the *Marriage*:

[53]   Does the Eagle know what is in the pit?
[54]   Or wilt thou go ask the Mole?

The answer (given in *Visions of the Daughters of Albion*) is that of the Alchemists:

> "Does not the eagle scorn the earth & despise the treasures beneath?
> But the mole knoweth what is there, & the worm shall tell it thee.
> Does not the worm erect a pillar in the mouldering church yard
> And a palace of eternity in the jaws of the hungry grave?"

[55] In *The Gates of Paradise* we see a figure in a shroud, wearing the winding-sheet and encircled by the worm, and below her the words, "I have said to the Worm: Thou art my mother & my sister." In 1788 Blake wrote in the margin of an aphorism by Lavater, which expresses contempt for the natural creation, "It is the God in *all* that is our companion & friend, for our God himself says: 'you are my brother, my sister & my mother'. . . . God is in the lowest effects as well as in the highest causes; for he is become a worm that he may nourish the weak."

[56]   This is the philosophy taught to Thel by the matron Clay, who speaks as "that which is beneath"—matter:

> "Thou seest me the meanest thing, and so I am indeed.
> My bosom of itself is cold, and of itself is dark;
> But he, that loves the lowly, pours his oil upon my head,
> And kisses me, and binds his nuptial bands around my breast,
> And says: 'Thou mother of my children, I have loved thee
> And I have given thee a crown that none can take away.'"

—the marriage of heaven and earth, the highest with the lowest. Paracelsus writes of the relation of the star-souls above to the bodily creatures below; in the beginning, he says, the upper heaven or stars and the inferior terrestrial nature were but one thing; but "God separated the subtle from the gross," the superior masculine from the inferior feminine watery nature; but there remains a concordance and "the things beneath are so [57] related to the things above as Man and Wife." The title-page of the *Marriage* illustrates this Paracelsian theme; many pairs of spirits meet in loving embrace, and the female comes from the dark abyss to meet the male, who descends from "above" on a bank of cloud.

But the divine principle "beneath" is a prisoner, whose release is the "great work" of the Alchemists. Vaughan, following Paracelsus, writes that "Heaven here below differs not from that above but in her captivity, and that above differs not from that below but in her liberty. The one is imprisoned in the matter, the other freed from all the grossness and impurities of it, but they are both one and the same nature, so that they easily unite"; and he concludes with an image that reminds us of matron Clay, "and hence it is that the Superior descends to the Inferior to visit and comfort her, in this sickly infectious habitation." "He, that loves the lowly," of whom the Clay speaks, and who pours "oil" upon her head, as the bride is anointed in the Jewish marriage-ceremony, is the Heavenly Father considered as husband of the Earthly Mother; and as matron Clay is given a "crown," so Vaughan writes that the stars "shed down their golden locks, like so many bracelets and tokens of their love."

Earth's traditional attributes, according to the Alchemists, are cold, moisture, and darkness, as both Paracelsus and Vaughan write; and Blake's matron Clay speaks of herself as "cold" and "dark," like Vaughan's matter, "a horrible confused qualm of stupefying spirit of moisture, cold, and darkness." This is the feminine principle or "Adamic earth"; and when Blake writes, in the *Marriage*, "Red clay brought forth," he is summarizing the teaching of Paracelsus; for all colours, Paracelsus says, are latent in her darkness; and Vaughan, "what rare pearls are there in this dunghill? . . . A pure eternal green overspreads her. . . . Roses red and white, golden lilies, azure violets, the bleeding Hyacinth, with their several celestial odours and spices." This is the wilderness that in Blake's *Marriage* is about to blossom as the rose, and Lyca's "desart wild" that is to "become a garden mild." Vaughan describes the Father "filling his powerful hands" and saying "Receive from me, O Holy Earth! that art ordained to be the Mother of all, lest thou shouldest want anything; when presently opening such hands as it becomes a God to have, he pour'd down all that was necessary for the constitution of things."

Paracelsus and, though less splendidly, Vaughan, studied and practised Alchemy as a means to practical ends; to Boehme it was a symbolic language purely and simply; his theme was the divine essence, good and evil, Heaven and Hell. In Boehme's writings the fire-principle is the Father, source of nature, and, as he repeats in countless passages, the abyss of Hell. From the fire proceeds the light, the Son, the principle of heaven; yet fire and light spring from a single root: "For the God of the holy World, and the God of the dark World, are not two Gods; there is but one only God." It is on the authority of Boehme that Blake wrote of the Jehovah of the Bible as "no other than he who dwells in flaming fire." This fire is Boehme's first principle of the Divine Essence. It is, in Blake's words, "Energy, call'd Evil," and in its fires the devils dwell, as "living Spirits in the Essences of the Eternal Original," as angels live in the principle of light; and each spirit is confined within its own principle. The devils can never enter Paradise; and yet, says Boehme, it has "no Wall of Earth or Stones about it, but there is a Great Gulph (or Cliff) between Paradise and this World, so that they who will pass from thence, thither, cannot; and they who would come to us cannot neither."

58]   *The Marriage of Heaven and Hell* shows a "mighty Devil" in his fires, his energies chained within his own principle as he vainly attempts to advance towards an angel who stands in the light. But the opposite of this is also true. Blake writes in the same "Memorable Fancy," "As I was walking among the fires of hell, delighted with the enjoyments of Genius, which to Angels look like torment and insanity . . ."; for energy—or, as Boehme also calls the fire-principle, desire—is "Eternal Delight"; and in "The Voice of the Devil" he says, "It indeed appear'd to Reason as if Desire was cast out; but the Devil's account is, that the Messiah fell, & form'd a heaven of what he stole from the Abyss."

[59] The energies of the abyss are the "Giants who formed this world into its sensual existence, and now seem to live in it in chains. . . ."

Orc, Blake's "frowning Babe," the Messiah of the New Age, comes from the Abyss, as his name (akin to Orcus, or Hell)
[60] implies. Blake depicts him always in his flames, the fire-principle to which he belongs; "the Eternal Hell revives." From the same rich context of Alchemical paradox arises the great unanswered question of "The Tyger," "Did he who made the Lamb make thee?"

Tigers and other savage beasts were a fashionable subject of painting at the end of the eighteenth century, an aspect of the Romantic revolt of evil, or energy. The vogue was introduced in
[61] England by Stubbs, whose famous tiger, now in the Tate Gallery, was exhibited at the Society of Artists of Great Britain, in Somerset Street, in 1769. Blake was then a boy of twelve years old, in his second year at Pars's drawing-school, held in the same house. Is there, in "The Tyger," an echo of a boy's enthusiasm for Stubbs's glorious beast?

One of Blake's "Proverbs of Hell" seems to relate the Tyger to Boehme's "wrath-fires" of the Father; "The tygers of wrath are wiser than the horses of instruction." But in his *Aurora* Boehme writes that evil beasts were never intended in the divine plan, and originated with the corruption of the world by Lucifer and his fallen angels. If there had been no Fall, there would have been no serpents, toads, or venomous insects; but when Lucifer exalted himself, and corrupted the fountains of creation, then the life-principle took on forms of evil, "as a fiery serpent, or Dragon, and imaged and framed all manner of fiery and poisonous Forms and Images, like to wild, cruel and evil Beasts"; for Lucifer, says Boehme, "half killed, spoiled and destroyed" the source of life; so the beast "which had most of the Fire, or the bitter, or the astringent quality became also a bitter, hot and fierce beast."

From many passages in Blake's longer poems it seems that the Tyger is an embodiment of evil; and a corruption of humanity; tigers and lions are called "dishumaniz'd men," and

> . . . the Tyger fierce
> Laughs at the human form. . . .

As Lyca in the Lion's den was met by animal forms, so in the world "beneath" those who have lost the vision of eternity become mere human animals;

> Troop by troop the beastial droves rend one another. . . .
>   . . . those that remain
> Return in pangs & horrible convulsions to their beastial state;
> For the monsters of the Elements, Lions or Tygers or Wolves,
> Sound loud the howling music . . . terrific men
> They seem to one another, laughing terrible among the
>   banners.

These "monsters of the Elements" do not belong to the world of the divine logos, nor to the primal fire-principle, but to error or creation; and "Error, or Creation, will be Burned up, & then, & not till Then, Truth or Eternity will appear. It is Burnt up the Moment Men cease to behold it." It is, Blake says, a "most pernicious Idea" to believe that "before the Creation All was Solitude and Chaos"; for, as Plato also taught, all things exist in "their Eternal Forms" in the divine mind. But in this world of illusion, there are "horrid shapes & sights of torment"; men are metamorphosed into serpents—that is to say, fall into the power of the serpent, matter. In the caves and dens of this world, we meet "the terrors of the Abyss," serpents and scorpions, and beasts of prey. Lamb and child live in the vision of eternity the world of "Jesus the Imagination"; but the Tyger roams "the forests of the night," removed from the light of the spiritual sun.

Forests, in Blake's symbolic landscape, represent creation and are always evil. Vala, the Shadowy Female, roams "In forests of eternal death, shrieking in hollow trees"; there blind Tiriel and his serpent-haired daughter wander "to the covert of a wood . . . where wild beasts resort . . . but from her cries the tygers fled." Everywhere we find the same image combined—darkness, forests, beasts of prey; and with forests we find associated images of smoke and fire.

In this association Blake is following Paracelsus, who likens nature, the "great mystery," to a forest that burns as it grows, issuing from nothing and returning to nothing again, "as a forest which the fire burneth into a little heap of ashes . . . such is the beginning, such is the end of the creatures." So Blake's lions and tigers "roam in the redounding smoke, in forests of affliction," the ever-growing, ever-consuming mystery of nature. The forests and their creatures are themselves the smoke, for as Paracelsus writes: "All bodies shall pass away and vanish into nothing but smoke, they shall all end in a fume." Thus Vala, as Nature, is called "the demoness of smoke"; and in the Last Judgment, Mystery, who is both goddess and tree, is burned up:

In the fierce flames the limbs of Mystery lay consuming. . . .
. . . The tree of Mystery went up in folding flames.

In his painting of the Last Judgment Blake describes a group of

figures representing "the Eternal Consummation of Vegetable
62] Life & Death with its Lusts. The wreathed Torches in their
hands represents Eternal Fire which is the fire of Generation or
Vegetation; it is an Eternal Consummation." But the symbol is
more ancient than Paracelsus; it is Heraclitus' image of the
earth as a great fire, parts kindling, parts going out; Yeats too
writes

> A tree there is that from its topmost bough
> Is half all glittering flame and half all green. . . . .

As with all great symbols, the burning tree of Nature is, as Blake
says, permanent in the human imagination.

So Blake's Tyger "burning bright" is itself part of the ever-
burning ever-consuming forest of nature. Blake's Nameless
Shadowy Female (nameless surely because she is the Great Mys-
tery itself) speaks of her children as a "progeny of fires"; in "The
Tyger" Blake asks

> What the hand dare sieze the fire?

and in the poem "Europe" we are given a possible answer; for
the Shadowy Female seizes the fire of the stars above in order to
generate creatures in the nether abyss, according to the Alchem-
ical teaching of the concordance of the stars with the natural
creation:

> "Unwilling I look up to heaven, unwilling count the stars:
> Sitting in fathomless abyss of my immortal shrine
> I sieze their burning power
> And bring forth howling terrors, all devouring fiery kings,
>
> Devouring & devoured, roaming on dark and desolate
>   mountains,
> In forests of eternal death, shrieking in hollow trees.

Ah mother Enitharmon!

[63]   Stamp not with solid form this vig'rous progeny of fires.

I bring forth from my teeming bosom myriads of flames. . . ."

Is not the Tyger "burning bright" one of this "progeny of fires,"
the "all devouring fiery kings," "Consumed and consuming" in
the "immortal shrine" in the abyss, immortal as darkness and
matter, the eternal opposite of light and spirit?

Another Alchemical symbol has become partly obscured in
the final draft of the poem, "The Tyger," which reads

In what distant deeps or skies
Burnt the fire of thine eyes?
On what wings dare he aspire?

But a cancelled draft in Blake's notebook brings out the contrast
of above and beneath:

Burnt in distant deeps or skies
The cruel fire of thine eyes?
Could heart descend or wings aspire?

—did the Creator draw his Tyger forth from Heaven or Hell? In
the final draft Blake has implied an identity of the deeps and the
skies; but unless we realize that his starting-point is their oppos-
ition, we shall miss the force of the paradox, which suggests that
Heaven and Hell may be, after all, aspects of the One Thing.
Thomas Vaughan paraphrases the Smaragdine Table.

Heaven above, heaven beneath,
Stars above, stars beneath,
All that is above is also beneath.
Understand this and be happy.

But the figure who seizes the fire to create the Tyger is male; and while we may conclude a resemblance and affinity with the Shadowy Female we must look farther.

> On what wings dare he aspire?
> What the hand dare sieze the fire?

The theft of fire suggests Prometheus; the daring aspiration, Satan, who in *The Marriage of Heaven and Hell* "formed a heaven with what he stole from the Abyss"—the flaming fires of the Father. Whoever made the Tyger cannot have been the Son or Logos, for he is a thief and a rebel, who in order to create must possess himself of fires not his own. Crabb Robinson, Wordsworth's friend, the diarist, recalls Blake as saying—and he had Wordsworth in mind—that "whoever believes in Nature disbelieves in God—for Nature is the work of the Devil. On my [Robinson] obtaining from him [Blake] the declaration that the Bible was the word of God, I referred to the commencement of *Genesis*—in the beginning God created the Heavens and the Earth. But I gained nothing by this, for I was triumphantly told that this God was not Jehovah, but the Elohim, and the doctrine of the Gnostics repeated with sufficient consistency to silence one so unlearned as myself."

Blake he calls a Gnostic; and it is quite possible that Blake did know something of the Gnostics from the writings of Joseph Priestley and elsewhere. Common to all schools of Gnosticism is the belief that the creator of the temporal world was not the supreme God; and among Jewish Gnostics, the Creator of Genesis is identified with this second creator. Blake's Urizen is recognizably the God of the Old Testament; grey-bearded and venerable in his "aged ignorance," he carries with him the Books of the Law. In Blake's *Job* we see him as the author of the Ten Commandments; but that he also is the Devil we know from his cloven foot. Yet Blake's creator is not wholly evil; for as the

Ancient of Days we see the Creator with his golden compasses, like the demiurge of the Gnostics who, though in part fallen, "derived his birth from the supreme god; this being fell, by degrees, from his native virtue, and his primitive dignity." But whatever grandeur there may be in his work, Blake called the creator of the temporal world "a very cruel being."

Paracelsus too wrote of "another creator of the mysteries, besides the chiefest and most high"; for the creatures, he says, "are always egged on and provoked to do evill, compelled thereto by the fates, stars, and by the infernal one; which by no means could have bin, if they had proceeded out of the most high himself, that we should be forced into these properties of good and evil."

[66]   Two poems in *Songs of Experience*, "The Human Abstract" and "A Poison Tree," identify the Tree of Good and Evil as mystery, or Nature: Mystery bears

> . . . the fruit of Deceit
> Ruddy and sweet to eat;

and the Poison Tree "an apple bright" that slays the man who eats it. The Poison Tree grows from "wrath" and the "apple bright" from anger; and we are led, again, to Boehme. For Boehme also this Tree is Nature: "it grew out of the Earth and has wholly the Nature of the Earth in it" and "as the earth is corruptible, and shall pass away in the End, when all goes into its Ether." He might be paraphrasing Paracelsus. Of the two trees in the old legend—the Tree of Life and the Tree of Good and Evil— Boehme writes that they are the same tree, but manifested in two different principles: in the light of Heaven, the principle of the Son; and in the fires of Hell, the "wrath of the anger of God," the

[67]   Father. Adam, who might have lived upon the "fruits of life"— Blake too uses the phrase—chose instead the earthly nature of the tree. The words "wrath," "poison," and "anger" that recur

in these two poems point unmistakably to Boehme, who writes that "the Tree, corrupted by the Fall, brought forth Fruits, according to its comprehensible, palpable, hard, evil, wrathful, poisonous, venomous, half-dead kind"; and he asks that human question, "*Why* did God suffer this Tree to grow, seeing Man should eat it? Did he not bring it forth for the fall of Man? And must it not be the Cause of Man's Destruction?" In Blake's Poison Tree

> . . . my wrath did grow. . . .
> And it grew both day and night
> Till it bore an apple bright. . . .

The figured man who lies outstretched in death beneath the tree is, by implication, the victim of God's anger. This myth is expanded in *The Four Zoas*; not only do poisonous fruits grow from the tree, but the serpent itself issues from "writhing buds." From this "deadly root" of poison and wrath the Mystery branches and extends endlessly,

> In intricate labyrinths o'erspreading many a grizly deep

—those "labyrinths" of nature, where Enion hid herself.

Man's "Mortal part" is the cruel work of nature and vanishes with the Mystery; on the Laocoön Group he wrote, "What can be Created can be Destroyed. Adam is only the Natural Man & not the Soul or Imagination"; he is created from the "red clay"; and the Tyger also is moulded in clay:

68]
69]

> In what clay & in what mould
>   Were thy eyes of fury roll'd?

Man as a clay vessel moulded by a potter is a Biblical metaphor; but those grand images of the moulding of the Tyger,

> And what shoulder, & what art
> Could twist the sinews of thy heart?
> And when thy heart began to beat
> What dread hand? & what dread feet?

lead us also to another source. The Fifth Book of the *Hermetica*, that source-book of the Alchemical philosophy, is written in praise of the demiurge; the Pymander here describes the cunning of the Workman who frames man in the womb:

> Who circumscribed and marked out his eyes? Who bored his nostrils and ears? Who opened his mouth, who stretched out and tied together his sinews? Who channelled the veins? Who hardened and made strong the bones? Who clothed the flesh with skin? Who divided the fingers and the joints? Who flatted and made broad the soles of the feet? Who digged the pores? Who stretched out the spleen, who made the heart like a Pyramis?

Even the rhetoric—those questions that in being asked are answered—is that of Blake's poem; the twisting of the sinews, the eyes "circumscribed and marked out," the flattening of the broad soles of the feet, the heart "like a Pyramis," with its suggestion of πυρ, Blake's "furnace." The association of "Nostrils, Eyes & Ears" recurs in later poems. In Urizen's "dens" the "dishumaniz'd men" are called tigers, lions, serpents, and monsters; and this same image describes the closing of their senses:

> . . . their Ears
> Were heavy & dull, & their eyes & nostrils closed up.

In the poem "To Tirzah" it is again the female principle who is held responsible for this binding:

> Thou, Mother of my Mortal part
> With cruelty didst mould my Heart,
> And with false self-decieving tears
> Didst bind my Nostrils, Eyes & Ears:
>
> Didst close my Tongue in senseless clay,
> And me to Mortal Life betray.

The workman of the Tyger (so we may deduce from early drafts of the poem) is both potter and blacksmith; he moulds the eyes in clay, but he also works with hammer, anvil, and furnaces.

> What the hammer? What the chain?
> In what furnace was thy brain?
> What the anvil? what dread grasp
> Dare its deadly terrors clasp?

[70] Blake's Los, the time-spirit, is also both potter and blacksmith; he beats out in heart-beats on his anvil the chains of time; and he is master also of ". . . the Potter's Furnace among the Funeral Urns of Beulah"—the male's "Furnace of beryll" associated with the looms of the Naiades; for the funeral urns which he moulds are the mortal bodies—an image also found in the Hermetica that leads us back to the bowls or urns of Porphyry's cave. But Los's famous furnaces belonged first to Urizen the demiurge:

> Then Los with terrible hands siez'd on the Ruin'd Furnaces
> Of Urizen: Enormous work, he builded them anew,
> Labour of Ages. . . .

They were "Ruin'd" by the demiurge, at the beginning of creation; and again we are pointed back to Boehme and the corrupting of the source. Los the time-spirit must labour to rebuild what was ruined in the beginning—enormous work indeed. The Hermetic workman was called "god of the fire, and the Spirit"; for "the Mind which is the Workman of all, useth the fire as his instrument." It is the demiurge who seizes the fire; and now it is the time-spirit of evolution who must labour to restore what was lost in the beginning. Los's "Labour of Ages" is the traditional work of Alchemy, to perfect the creation in the resurrection of the hidden god.

The Furnaces of Los are seven in number; so are Boehme's qualifying spirits, or fountains; and the identity of the furnaces with these fountains we know, because at the end of the time-process their original purity is restored:

> . . . the Furnaces became
> Fountains of Living Waters flowing from the Humanity Divine.

[71] But there are also seven planetary spirits; Plato describes them turning round the Spindle of Necessity: seven *elohim*, or creators, [72] in the Jewish mystical tradition, retained as the sevenfold gifts of the Holy Ghost in Christianity. Los's furnaces retain also a strange affinity with the planetary spheres; for they are "Seven-fold each within other," like Plato's Spindle of Necessity. Para-celsus compares the whole created world to a furnace "wherein the Seeds of the Sun and Moon, by their various astral influences are corrupted and concocted and digested, for the Generation of all things." Los's furnace is the *Athanor* of the Alchemists, built, as Paracelsus says, "in imitation of the Foundation of Heaven and Earth," where the Alchemist labours at the great work in which nature also, as St. Paul says, "groans and travails" towards redemption.

Whenever Blake writes of the stars he understands them as the planetary rulers of destiny. Urizen he calls "the Starry King," or as Satan, "Prince of the Starry Wheels," "Starry Jealousy," and leader of the "starry hosts." The Zoas he calls "immortal starry

ones." They are "the Starry Eight," the seven planets, and the
eighth sphere of the fixed stars, ruled by Urizen. (Boehme's God
73] the Father is also described as ruler of the firmament; and if he
can be likened to anything, Boehme says, it is "to the round
74] Globe of Heaven.") Los, who is called "the fourth immortal
starry one," is given the traditional number of the sun, proper to
his solar nature, throughout the Prophetic Books.

Souls who enter the created world from beyond the galaxy
become subject to the demiurge. In the "Introduction" to Songs of
Experience Blake reminds the fallen soul that she herself comes
from eternity, and

> . . . might controll
> The starry pole
> And fallen, fallen light renew!

But in this world she is subject to "Starry Jealousy," who, like
the Hermetic demiurge, "containing the Circles and Whirling
them about, turned round on a Wheel his own Workmanships
and suffered them to be turned from an indefinite Beginning to
an undeterminable end."

Thus prepared, we can turn to the stars as they appear in "The
Tyger."

> When the stars threw down their spears,
> And water'd heaven with their tears,
> Did he smile his work to see?

In The Four Zoas Urizen himself recalls the same event:

> . . . I hid myself in black clouds or my wrath;
> I call'd the stars around my feet in the night of councils dark;
> The stars threw down their spears & fled naked away.
> We fell. I siezed thee, dark Urthona. In my left hand falling

> I siez'd thee, beauteous Luvah; thou art faded like a flower
> And like a lilly is thy wife Vala wither'd by winds.

The stars who threw down their spears when the demiurge fell are the same as the stars in "The Tyger"; they are the planets, [75] Blake's Zoas, the energies of the human soul, some of whom are here named. As in all traditional accounts of the Fall, the demiurge draws down with him the planetary spirits whom he governs.

The throwing down of the spears echoes Milton's account of the same event, the fall of the rebel angels, driven out of heaven by Messiah's chariot:

> . . . they astonisht all resistance lost,
> All courage; down thir idle weapons drop'd;
> O're Shields and Helmes, and helmed heads he rode. . . .

They flee,

> . . . witherd all thir strength,
> And of thir wonted vigour left them draind,
> Exhausted, spiritless, afflicted, fall'n

—as Luvah and Vala are faded and wither'd. It is these same stars whom in illustrating the Book of Job Blake has shown in their renewed brightness,

> When the morning stars sang together, and
> all the sons of God shouted for joy.

What, then, in the light of all this, is the answer we are to give to the final question of "The Tyger?" "Did he who made the Lamb make thee?" Are we to answer it in Boehme's words:

> The God of the holy World, and the God of the dark World, are

> not two Gods; there is but one only God. He himself is all
> Being. He is Evil and Good; Heaven and Hell; Light and Dark-
> ness; Eternity and Time. Where His Love is hid in anything,
> there His Anger is manifest.

This is the god of the Alchemists, beyond the contraries. But the answer of the Platonists, and of the *Hermetica*, would be No: the Tyger belongs to the fallen time-world. Yet on the deepest level, all these traditions converge, for the time-world exists only by divine permission. Blake, I believe, left his great question unanswered not because he was in doubt, but because the only answer is a No and Yes of such depth and complexity.

Nor must we overlook, in analyzing the meaning of the text, all that is conveyed by the powerful exaltation of the metre, by the fiery grandeur of the images. If the discoverable meaning of the poem suggests that the Tyger is the work of a creator ambiguous or evil, the emotive force of metre and image is all affirmation, praising the fiery might, the energy, and the intelligence of the mortal God. "The Tyger" is preparing the way for the *Marriage*, with its vindication of Hell or Energy:

> The roaring of lions, the howling of wolves, the raging of the
> stormy sea, and the destructive sword, are portions of eternity,
> too great for the eye of man.

Instead of seeking to find a Yes or a No, we will be nearest to the truth if we see "The Tyger" rather as an utterance of Blake's delight, not in the solution, but in the presentation of the problem of evil as he found it in the Hermetic and Alchemical tradition.

PROPHET AGAINST SCIENCE

Blake as a neo-Platonist, Blake as an enthusiast for the philosophy of Alchemy—how is this picture to be reconciled with that other Blake of whom Bronowski, Erdman, and other scholars have written, the man passionately engaged in the philosophic and political issues of his own time? The more deeply we study him the more clearly we see how the wisdom he learned from remote sources was brought to bear on problems near at hand.

[76]   Bacon, Newton, and Locke are but the names under which he denounced the scientific philosophy which still continues to dominate the modern West. When in 1808 he annotated, with devastating comments, his copy of Reynolds' *Discourses on Painting*, he recalled that when young he had read Burke's treatise which "is founded on the Opinions of Newton," Locke *On Human Understanding*, and Bacon's *Advancement of Learning*: "I felt the Same Contempt & Abhorrence then that I do now. They mock Inspiration & Vision. Inspiration & Vision was then, & now is, & I hope will always Remain, my Element, my Eternal Dwelling place. . . ."

His first engraved plates are a series of three short tractates

[77] entitled *There Is No Natural Religion* and *All Religions Are One*; and in these we find a reasoned refutation of the philosophy of Locke. Locke argues that there are no innate ideas in the mind, and all we know comes through sense-impressions—a foreshadowing of behaviourism. Blake summarizes his argument:

> Man has no notion of moral fitness but from Education. Naturally he is only a natural organ subject to Sense.

How different is this view from Blake's conception of the child we know from *Songs of Innocence*, and from those many depic-
[78] tions of the Child Jesus; Blake's children are not natural organs awaiting the imprints of sense, but life itself. It is imagination, not the senses, that is able

> To see a World in a Grain of Sand
>   And a Heaven in a Wild Flower,
> Hold Infinity in the palm of your hand
>   And Eternity in an hour.

The mental experience is all we know with certainty; and Blake concludes his arguments against Locke with an affirmation of "the true Man," or "the Poetic Genius," as omnipresent mind.

Blake's phrase "the true Man" again leads us to Taylor—to another essay in those volumes of Proclus' *Commentaries on Euclid* in which Blake read Porphyry's *On the Cave of the Nymphs*—*A Dissertation on the Platonic Doctrine of Ideas*. "The true man, both according to Aristotle and Plato, is intellect," says Taylor; and indeed we find in this essay most of the arguments Blake brings against Bacon, Newton, and Locke. "According to Mr. Locke," Taylor writes, "the soul is a mere *tabula rasa*, an empty recipient, a mechanical blank. According to Plato she is an ever-written tablet, a plenitude of forms, a vital and intellectual energy. On the former system, she is on a level with the most degraded natures, the receptacle of material species, and the spectator of delusion and non-entity." He joins the names of Blake's other arch-enemies, Bacon and Newton, calling Newton a great mathematician but no philosopher. He calls the philosophies of all three "self-taught systems"; and such, by the standards of the Perennial Philosophy, of course they are.

The traditional doctrine of an indwelling divine mind Blake knew in many versions besides the Platonic: it is a central teaching in the *Hermetica*; he knew the *Bhagvat-Geeta*. "Mr. Wilkin translating the Geeta" is the subject of a lost painting; and he must also have known the writings and translations of Sir William Jones, the orientalist. Jones actually points out the resemblance of the Hindu philosophy that sees all phenomena as *maya*, a system of appearances whose only reality is in mind, to the philosophy of Berkeley. Blake too considered the Divine Imagination to be present in all men—indeed in all creatures.

It is because the Jewish tradition is supremely prophetic and imaginative (as against the rational thought of Greece) that Blake sees the "jews' god" as finally triumphant; for the indwelling imagination that spoke by the prophets is at last manifested as "the divine Humanity," "Jesus the Imagination."

Swedenborg, the Alchemists, and the entire European esoteric tradition see the outward form as the signature, or correspondence of the informing mind, or life: a view that anticipates Teilhard de Chardin's view of the "within" of nature that is inseparable from the "without"; and Blake defends this view, not only of man but of all creatures:

> "With what sense is it that the chicken shuns the ravenous hawk?
> With what sense does the tame pigeon measure out the expanse?

With what sense does the bee form cells? have not the mouse
   & frog
Eyes and ears and sense of touch? yet are their habitations
And their pursuits as different as their forms and as their joys.
Ask the wild ass why he refuses burdens, and the meek camel
Why he loves man: is it because of eye, ear, mouth, or skin,
Or breathing nostrils? No, for these the wolf and tyger have.
Ask the blind worm the secrets of the grave, and why her spires
Love to curl round the bones of death; and ask the rav'nous
   snake
Where she gets poison, & the wing'd eagle why he loves the
   sun;
And then tell me the thoughts of man, that have been hid of
   old."

The "hidden" thoughts of man are his share in the Divine Imagination—hidden, perhaps, as Jung has described the archetypes that determine our nature, because inaccessible to normal consciousness; they create us, not we them. Blake draws the [79] moral: "One Law for the Lion & Ox is Oppression."

All earlier versions of the opposing principles of ratio and vision, the natural Adam and Jesus the Imagination, Blake has simplified, in his great poem Milton, into the myth of "Satan the Selfhood" overcome by imagination. This selfhood, the mind of the ratio, is the only demiurge, and we ourselves the creators of our fallen world. The kingdom cut off from God proves to be neither more nor less than the universe of externality, especially as conceived by the scientific philosophy. Hell is the universe seen as a mechanism, and Satan is called "the spirit of the natural frame" and "Newton's Pantocrator, weaving the Woof of Locke"—*maya* wrongly conceived as substantial reality. Those "dark Satanic Mills" which have aroused so much speculation are the Newtonian universe, "a mill with complicated wheels"; and the landscape of industrialism is but the shadow of the philosophy which has produced it. Blake re-tells Milton's theme of Satan's fall and assumption of power, but his Satan is the mind of the ratio, the scientific mentality which had, according to Blake, infected even Milton, friend of Galileo, with the erroneous philosophy of his age.

[80]   Satan unfallen we see in a painting "Lucifer before the Fall." His externality Blake has conveyed in his masklike appearance, as of a puppet—for such the selfhood is, a mere play upon the surface of ever-mysterious life. Blake uses of the selfhood a Swedenborgian term: it is "a form & organ of life," upheld only by divine influx (another Swedenborgian term). Lucifer is surrounded by fairies of the four elements, signifying that his rule is over "nature," externality—the phenomena. His story as it is told in *Milton* is complicated by the introduction of Calvin's terms of the Elect, the Redeemed, and the Reprobate; Blake uses these terms because Milton employed them in *Paradise Lost*.

> . . . the Class of Satan shall be call'd the Elect, & those
> Of Rintrah the Reprobate, & those of Palamabron the Redeem'd:
> For he is redeem'd from Satan's Law. . . .

In saying that Satan is the type of the Elect, Blake is not merely indulging in Chestertonian paradox; for Calvin defined the Elect as those who live by the will and grace of God at every moment, as the forms and organs of life are upheld by spiritual influx; Satan, as externality and appearance only,

> . . . must be new Created continually moment by moment
> And therefore the Class of Satan shall be call'd the Elect. . . .

The Reprobate "never cease to Believe"—to believe, that is, in the imagination—while the Redeemed "live in doubts & fears perpetually tormented by the Elect. . . ." Jesus the Imagination is continually born among the Reprobate—

He died as a Reprobate, he was Punish'd as a Transgressor

—for imagination is reprobate by the ruler of this world, the mind of the ratio. This theme Blake had already stated in the *Marriage*, where a "Devil" praises Jesus as the breaker of all the ten commandments, because He was "all virtue, and acted from impulse, not from rules"; and he returned to it long after in "The Everlasting Gospel," to ask whether Jesus was humble, or chaste, or possessed any of the moral virtues, answering again in the negative; for the imagination has other laws.

In *Milton* Blake has attempted to convey the mystery of these laws in the myth of Satan's exchange of tasks with Palamabron, 81] type of the Reprobate. It is Palamabron's task to guide the Harrow of Shaddai

A Scheme of Human conduct invisible & incomprehensible.

Satan guides the Mills, the "Starry Wheels" of the Newtonian universe, by the scientific laws of mechanistic causality. Satan (still in his "youth and beauty," as he is in the painting of unfallen Lucifer) pleads with Los, the time-spirit, to allow him to exchange tasks with Palamabron. He argues that scientific reason ought to control human conduct; therefore let Palamabron take "the easier task" of ordering the natural universe and allow Satan, the mind of the Ratio, to exercise his talents where he feels (quite sincerely) that they can be employed most effectively. Reluctantly Los consents to the exchange, and rational morality becomes thenceforth the law of human conduct, while that which is above and beyond reason, ever-mysterious life, is brought under its control.

Palamabron's Harrow of Shaddai may be understood when we learn that Shaddai is the Hebrew Divine Name of the

Redeemer—who is, in Christian theology, Jesus, and therefore, in Blake's terms, the imagination. Turning to *Paradise Lost* we discover that the Redeemed are guided by the innate divine light:

> And I will place within them as a guide
> My Umpire *Conscience*, whom if they will hear,
> Light after light well us'd they shall attain,
> And to the end persisting, safe arrive.

Conscience, or imagination, is the Redeemer working in mankind.

[82]   In *Jerusalem* there is a representation of "the Plow of Jehovah and the Harrow of Shaddai"—one or the other, or both. The entire plow or harrow mentioned in the text is not shown in the design, but only the fore part, serpent-wheeled, and dragged by two man-headed, ox-hoofed, powerful creatures. Are these the "Horses of Palamabron"? Each has upon his head a single horn, coiled ram-like; they are in fact unicorns, of a sort. Each horn terminates in a hand. The hand on the left points the way; that on the right is directed backwards to receive a pen from one of two winged bird-headed creatures who ride the beasts; the chariot is alive with eagle and serpent, the mysteries of the "above" and the "beneath." The unicorn leads us to the Book of Job, where, as Blake says in *The Marriage of Heaven and Hell*, "Milton's Messiah is call'd Satan," and the divine nature is revealed as mysterious and incomprehensible to reason. Job is reconciled to the ways of God when he bows before the mystery. Of this mystery the unicorn is the type; he cannot be harnessed, like the "horses of instruction" who draw the chariot of Milton's false Messiah "or Reason," shown on a page of the *Marriage*, falling into the abyss with his horse and his chariot.

> Will the unicorn be willing to serve thee, or abide by thy crib?
> Canst thou bind the unicorn with his band in the furrow? or will

> he harrow the valleys after thee? . . . wilt thou leave thy labour
> to him . . ., that he will bring home thy seed . . .?

The unicorn is the horse of the Harrow of God; and in Rintrah
and Palamabron we have again those mysterious contraries of
good and evil which run through all human affairs.

This harrow, then, after repeated entreaties, Los the time-spirit
gives to the rationalist Satan. At the end of a "day"—a thousand
years are a day to God—

> . . . the horses of the Harrow
> Were madden'd with tormenting fury, & the servants of the
>   Harrow,
> The Gnomes, accus'd Satan with indignation, fury and fire.

Just as it was said of the earlier demiurge, Urizen, that no flesh
and blood could bear his laws one moment, so it is with the
"One Law for Lion and Ox" of Satan's externally imposed moral
code—a fact forced upon the notice of modern psychology, and
well known to Blake:

> . . . the strongest of Demons trembled,
> Curbing his living creatures; many of the strongest Gnomes
> They bit in their wild fury, who also madden'd like wildest
>   beasts.

This rebellion of the reason-curbed energies of life Blake con-
trasts with the joyous bacchanalia Palamabron has meanwhile
introduced in the world of nature.

> The servants of the Mills drunken with wine and dancing wild
> With shouts and Palamabron's songs, rending the forests
>   green
> With ecchoing confusion. . . .

—as wild creatures continue to do, to the continual envy and admiration of reason-fettered mankind.

Satan himself does not believe that he has oppressed the horses of the Harrow; knowing nothing of eternity he believes in his own rational laws; for he is by definition the puppet selfhood of externality, the ego, and as such cannot be redeemed. The poem *Milton* follows his course from his first "extreme Mildness" to the formulation of moral laws and the punishment of those who disobey them, plunging the world at last into war and destruction.

> "For Moral Virtues all begin
> In the Accusations of Sin,
> And all Heroic Virtues End
> In destroying the Sinners' Friend."

We are left in no doubt that Satan is the "God" of the Ten Commandments by the plate that shows the poet—"the inspired [83] man"—pulling down his image—a mere man-made idol—in the strength of imaginative inspiration. In the *Job* engravings Satan's most terrible disguise is in the shape of God, "like the [84] most high," but recognizable by his cloven foot.

> Tho' thou art Worship'd by the Names Divine
> Of Jesus & Jehovah, thou art still
> The Son of Morn in weary Night's decline,
> The lost Traveller's Dream under the Hill.

Blake's prophecies are addressed, specifically, to the English nation, the Giant Albion. *Vala, Milton,* and *Jerusalem* all tell of the fall of the national mind into the "deadly sleep" of the scientific philosophy of Bacon, Newton, and Locke; and our Prophet calls [85] the sleepers to reawaken to the vision of eternity. "Man anciently contain'd in his mighty limbs all things in Heaven &

Earth," but "in his Chaotic State of Sleep, Satan & Adam & the
[86] whole World was Created by the Elohim"; the world of nature,
originally a part of man himself, because part of his experience,
[87] has come, through the scientific philosophy, to seem as if sep-
arate from the soul; for "Mental Things are alone Real; what is
call'd Corporeal, Nobody Knows of its Dwelling Place: it is in
Fallacy, & its Existence an Imposture. Where is the Existence
Out of Mind or Thought? Where is it but in the Mind of a
Fool?" Blake is here paraphrasing Berkeley, and it is with full
understanding of the philosophic questions involved that he
writes

> . . . in your own Bosom you bear your Heaven
a,b] And Earth & all you behold; tho' it appears Without, it is
>   Within,
>   In your Imagination, of which this World of Mortality is but a
>   Shadow.

Unfallen Albion contains his world in his own soul. The refrain
that runs through *Milton* and *Jerusalem*:

> But now the Starry Heavens are fled from the mighty limbs of
>   Albion

is like writing on the tomb of a nation under the domination of
the positivist philosophy.

The sickness of Albion is the false belief that the phenomena
of nature have an existence apart from mind; thus he has lost part
of his soul, as Jung also has since said. At the same time the
phenomena, emptied of spiritual life, have become a desert of
dead particles. Blake returns again and again to the description of
this disease of the modern West; and he conceives it in two ways:
as the shrinking of man, and as the wandering away of the
creatures, who stray

> . . . over the four-fold wilderness:
> They return not, but generate in rocky places desolate:
> They return not, but build a habitation separate from Man. . . .
> As the Senses of Men shrink together under the Knife of flint
> In the hands of Albion's Daughters. . . .

He both depicts and describes the female powers externalizing sun, moon, and stars from the bodies of Albion's children:

> ". . . the Blue
> Of our immortal Veins & all their Hosts fled from our Limbs
> And wander'd distant in a dismal Night clouded & dark.
> The Sun fled from the Briton's forehead, the Moon from his
>   mighty loins. . . ."

It is the externalization of nature

> Which separated the stars from the mountains, the mountains
>   from Man
> And left Man, a little grovelling Root outside of Himself.

In *Vala* Blake was already using the sickness of Job as the type of the sickness of Albion. The Eternal Man is afflicted with Job's boils; he loses his children, and, like the nomadic Job, "his flocks & herds & tents & pastures," "Till he forgot eternity," Blake says; for the loss is an externalization:

> His inward Eyes closing from the Divine vision, & all
> His Children wand'ring outside, from his bosom fleeing away.

In *Jerusalem* again there are passages that leave no doubt that Blake was telling the story of Albion in terms of the story of Job; here again he is covered with the "boils" of deadly sin, and afterwards

"First fled my Sons & then my Daughters, then my Wild
  Animations,
My Cattle next, last ev'n the Dog of my Gate; the Forests fled
The Corn-fields & the breathing Gardens outside separated,
The Sea, the Stars, the Sun, the Moon, driv'n forth by my
  disease.
All is Eternal Death. . . ."

—for Albion is now dead to eternity, living in a world where even people have become mere things.

There can be no doubt therefore that when Blake began his last and greatest completed work he conceived the story of Job in terms of western man's fall from imaginative vision into the power of the scientific philosophy. As Albion fell from the Divine Bosom, so Job loses the vision of God through the agency of Satan the Selfhood; externalized, his children are dead to him, and his pastoral riches lost; for possession of riches is the imaginative power to enjoy, not the material power to purchase. As Albion's soul, Jerusalem, suffers with him, so does Job's wife; and the three comforters who give him evil counsel are the fallen Zoas, Urizen, Tharmas, and Luvah. These are described in *The Four Zoas* as Albion's friends, who "visit" him at his house and lament over his misfortunes. It is easy to see the characters of the Zoas in the faces of the three friends of Job,

Urizen cold & scientific, Luvah pitying & weeping,
Tharmas indolent & sullen.

Los, who tells Albion,

Three thou has slain. I am the Fourth: thou canst not destroy me

89] may be recognized in Elihu, who comes as a bringer of hope. Job raises his eyes for the first time as Elihu approaches, like the one unfallen Zoa, Los, who "kept the Divine Vision in time of trouble." In the reconciling vision the sleeping God within awakens, pointing out to Job the mysterious and incompréhensible energies of life, Behemoth and Leviathan. Sun, moon, and stars are no longer globes "rolling thro' Voidness," but spiritual beings; and in the imaginative vision, one and the same in all men, his family is restored. Far from exalting nature, the scientific exaltation of the phenomena robs them of their meaning and beauty; and conversely the recognition of the phenomena as a portion of the "Soul" regenerates and resurrects "nature." Blake's visions of Job are the direct outcome of the thought first formulated in the *Tractates* nearly forty years earlier. His prophetic urgency to preach to the English nation a return to spiritual vision, lost since the Renaissance, dictated Blake's choice of theme, first and last.

The fallen man is surrounded by symbols of the indefinite, as he sleeps his earth-sleep in the sea of time and space. Matter, the foundation of his mistaken philosophy, is the oozy rock on which he lies, "A Rocky fragment from Eternity hurl'd," the same fragment that in the *Marriage* was stolen by the false Messiah when he "formed a heaven of what he stole from the Abyss." His world is called a chaos; for without imagination—Plato's intellect—matter has no ordering principle, and Locke's famous sense-impressions can produce only "a fortuitous concourse of memorys accumulated and lost." Albion's rock is "Beneath the Furnaces & the starry Wheels," in that Cave where the women weave on stone looms, "Calling the Rocks Atomic Origins of Existence."

In contrast with this "Chaotic State of Sleep," the soul of man possesses the fourfold pattern of the "mandala" lately described [90] by Jung. The Zoas are the four faculties of the soul, sometimes represented as four faces, sometimes as four gates of a city. The soul of Albion, as Blake describes it in this city, symbolism, has a strange defect: one of the four gates is closed, that toward the

West, where lost Eden lies. In this symbol again Blake is stating the characteristic defect of the Western mentality, the loss of man's "circumference," the natural world, through its externalization. There are a few, Blake tells us, like himself, whose "Western Gates" are "open"; for these Paradise is regained; for man's lost paradise is his world and his body, perceived once more as "a portion of soul." "The artist is an inhabitant of that happy country; and . . . the world of vegetation and generation may expect to be opened again to Heaven, through Eden, as it was in the beginning." Blake called the scientific philosophy idolatry, for what is it but the worship of stocks and stones? Those who believe that matter is an agent whose activities direct the world are the only heathen who have ever been so blind as to "bow down to wood and stone";

> . . . Albion's sleep is not
> Like Africa's, and his machines are woven with his life.

Gilchrist in his *Life of William Blake* tells of an acquaintance showing him a copy of *The Mechanic's Magazine*. "Ah, Sir," Blake said, "these things we artists hate."

Blake's vision of the good life was pastoral, lived in imaginative harmony with nature. "I see Every thing I paint In This World," Blake wrote; ". . . to the Eyes of the Man of Imagination, Nature is Imagination itself. As a man is, So he Sees." This was the vision that he transmitted for a while to Palmer and Calvert and other young disciples of his old age.

In these lectures I have attempted to show that in his "visions," Blake was not, as has often been supposed, an eccentric in a traditional civilization. Mr. Eliot has accused him of "a certain meanness of culture" and a lack of that "Mediterranean gift of form which knows how to borrow, as Dante borrowed his theory of the soul; he must needs create a philosophy as well as a poetry." A culture which embraced Plato and Plotinus, the Bible and the *Hermetica*, English science and philosophy, the tradition of Alchemy, Gibbon and Herodotus, besides the body of English poetry—not to mention his equally wide knowledge of painting—can scarcely be called mean. "He was anything but sectarian or exclusive," Samuel Palmer recollected, "finding sources of delight throughout the whole range of art; while as a critic he was judicious and discriminating." Blake, like Dante, derived his knowledge of the soul from the ancients. He was a traditionalist in a society that had as a whole lapsed from tradition. To the modern reader he appears most original when he is least so, most cranky when he is communicating traditional doctrine, and most personal when his theme is metaphysical reality, expressed in canonical symbols. Yeats was perfectly aware of this, but evidently follows the old injunction not to divulge the mysteries, lest, as D. H. Lawrence also understood, people "knowing the formulae, without undergoing the experience that corresponds, should grow insolent and impious, thinking they have the all, when they have only an empty monkey-chatter. The esoteric knowledge will always be esoteric, since knowledge is an experience, not a formula." All the same, Blake wished to be understood, and knew that he would be fully understood only by those in possession of the traditional language of symbols.

Tradition, as Coomaraswamy has defined the word, means in accordance with truth, knowledge absolute; tradition is that whole body of canonical symbolic language in which such metaphysical knowledge is enshrined, and in which the prophets, theologians, poets, and artists have transmitted it through the ages. It is quite possible, therefore, for a whole society to depart from tradition, while a solitary individual, rejecting his historical inheritance and speaking in terms strange to his contemporaries, his predecessors, and his successors, may yet be traditional. Coomaraswamy therefore took a view of Blake opposite from Eliot's; he did not contrast Blake and Dante, but named them together as the two supremely traditional poets of Europe. With the rediscovery of ancient myths and symbols and some of their meaning, we have begun to realize how little we have understood in works long familiar.

SELECT BIBLIOGRAPHY

This relatively short list makes no pretense to include all the important books on Blake in the ever-growing literature on the many aspects of his work. A fuller bibliography is given in *Blake and Tradition*, the longer work from which these lectures were abstracted. For the rest, readers should consult the bibliographical works listed below. The theme of this book— Blake in relation to certain aspects of the esoteric tradition—covers only one side of his varied interests and activities as a man of his time. The works listed here relate, therefore, only to the theme of this book. I have given a somewhat full—though by no means exhaustive—list of source books certainly, or with strong presumption, known to Blake, in the field indicated. This I have considered necessary if only to give the reader some idea of the number of such works that were in fact available to him in little known, and until recently little regarded, areas of "lost knowledge."

I

A. *Blake Bibliographies*

A Bibliography of William Blake. By Geoffrey Keynes. New York (Grolier Club), 1921. Revised 1953.

A Blake Bibliography: Annotated Lists of Works, Studies, and Blakeana. By G. E. Bentley, Jr., and Martin K. Nurmi. Minneapolis (University of Minnesota Press) and London, 1964.

B. *Editions of the Written Works*

The Works of William Blake, Poetic, Symbolic, and Critical. Edited, with Lithographs of the Illustrated "Prophetic Books," and a Memoir and Interpretation, by Edwin J. Ellis and W. B. Yeats. London, 1893. 3 vols.

The Complete Writings of William Blake. With All the Variant Readings. Edited by Geoffrey Keynes. London and New York, 1957. This "Variorum" (bicentenary) edition is now the definitive edition, containing material previously unpublished. A new edition appeared in 1966, with a few corrections and amendments but otherwise identical with the 1957 edition, which remains the source for the texts quoted in the present work.

C. *Works Published Separately*

Entries marked * were engraved, printed, and published in small editions by Blake himself as specimens of "illuminated printing." Facsimile editions before 1900 are not listed.

Poetical Sketches (1783). Facsimile edition, London (Noel Douglas), 1926.

* *All Religions are One* (c. 1788–94). Facsimile edition, ed. Frederick Hollyer. London, 1926.

* *There is No Natural Religion* (c. 1788). Facsimile edition, ed. Philip Hofer, Cambridge (Mass.), 1948.

* *Songs of Innocence* (1789). Facsimile edition, London (Trianon Press), 1954.

* *The Book of Thel* (1789). Facsimile edition, ed. Frederick Hollyer. London, 1924. Another, London and New York, 1928. Another, London (Trianon Press), 1965.

Tiriel. Not printed in Blake's lifetime. Facsimile and transcript of the manuscript, and reproductions of the drawings, ed. G. E. Bentley, Oxford, 1967.

* *The Marriage of Heaven and Hell* (1790). Facsimile, with a Note by Max

Plowman, London and New York, 1927. Facsimile edition, London (Trianon Press), 1960.

The French Revolution: A Poem in Seven Books. Book the First (1791). Not published in Blake's lifetime; the only recorded copy is probably a proof.

* *Visions of the Daughters of Albion* (1793). Facsimile, with a Note by J. Middleton Murry, London and New York, 1932. Facsimile edition, London (Trianon Press), 1959.

* *America: A Prophecy* (1793). Color facsimile edition, with a Foreword by Ruthven Todd. New York (United Book Guild), 1947. Facsimile edition, London (Trianon Press), 1963.

For Children: The Gates of Paradise (1793). Facsimile edition, London (Trianon Press), 1968.

For the Sexes: The Gates of Paradise (1818). A revised issue of *For Children: The Gates of Paradise* (1793), with text added. Facsimile edition, London (Trianon Press), 1968.

* *Songs of Innocence and Experience.* Shewing the Two Contrary States of the Human Soul (1794). Facsimile edition, London (Trianon Press), 1955.

* *Europe: A Prophecy* (1794). Facsimile edition, London (Trianon Press), 1969.

* *The [First] Book of Urizen* (1794). With a Note by Dorothy Plowman, London and New York, 1929. Facsimile edition, London (Trianon Press), 1958.

* *The Song of Los* (1795). Facsimile edition, London (Trianon Press), in preparation.

* *The Book of Los* (1795).

William Blake's Vala: Blake's Numbered Text. Edited by H. M. Margoliouth. Oxford, 1956. The text of the original poem of this name, before the additions and alterations made to the manuscript now entitled *The Four Zoas.* It is included here to complete the corpus of Blake's original works.

Vala, or The Four Zoas. A Facsimile of the Manuscript, a Transcript of the Poem, and a Study of its Growth and Significance. By G. E. Bentley, Jr. Oxford, 1963. See also *Vala,* ed. H. M. Margoliouth, above.

* *The Book of Ahania* (1795). One copy only recorded. Facsimile edition, London (Trianon Press), 1973.

* *Milton* (1804 [? 1808]). Facsimile edition, London (Trianon Press), 1967.

* *Jerusalem: The Emanation of the Giant Albion* (1804–20). Facsimile edition, in color, London (Trianon Press), 1951; idem, black and white, 1955. A simplified version prepared and edited by W. R. Hughes, London, 1964.

Blake's Chaucer. The Canterbury Pilgrims, The Fresco Picture, Representing Chaucer's Characters painted by William Blake, as it is now submitted to the Public, the Designer proposes to engrave, etc. [A prospectus]. (1809).

A *Descriptive Catalogue of Pictures*, Poetical and Historical Inventions, Painted by William Blake, in Water Colours, being the Ancient method of Fresco Painting Restored: and Drawings, for Public Inspection ... (1809). Compiled by Blake for an exhibition of his work.

The Notebook of William Blake Called the Rossetti Manuscript. Edited by Geoffrey Keynes. London, 1935. With facsimile.

Blake also designed and engraved illustrations for a number of books by other authors. Of these only those most relevant to the present work are listed.

Lavater's Aphorisms on Man. Translated from the original MS. of John Caspar Lavater. (Engraved by Blake.) London, 1788.

Salzmann, C. G. *Elements of Morality, for the Use of Children; with an Introductory Address to Parents*. (Translated from the German by Mary Wollstonecraft.) London, 1790, 2 vols. 2nd edn. (first with plates adapted by Blake from German originals), London, 1791, 3 vols.

Wollstonecraft, Mary. *Original Stories from Real Life*. London, 1791. Edited by E. V. Lucas, London, 1906.

Darwin, Erasmus. *The Botanic Garden*. A Poem. London, 1791. (Title-page of second part dated 1790.)

Cumberland, George. *Thoughts on Outline, Sculpture and the System that Guided the Ancient Artists in Composing their Figures and Groupes*. London, 1796.

Young, Edward. *Night Thoughts*. Edited by R. Edwards. London, 1797. See also *Illustrations to Young's Night Thoughts, Done in Water-Colour by William Blake*. Thirty pages reproduced from the original water colors in the library of W. White. With an introductory essay by Geoffrey Keynes. Cambridge (Mass.) and London, 1927.

Blair, Robert. *The Grave*. Illustrated by twelve etchings executed by Louis Schiavonetti from original inventions [of William Blake]. London, 1808. Reissued 1813; London, 1903; London, 1905. See also: *Blake's Grave: A Prophetic Book*. Being William Blake's illustrations for Robert Blair's *The Grave*, arranged as Blake directed. With a commentary by S. F. Damon, Providence, Rhode Island, 1953.

Thornton, Robert John. *The Pastorals of Virgil*. London, 1821. 2 vols. (This edition is the first with Blake's woodcuts.) Also edited by Laurence Binyon, London, 1902. See also *The Illustrations of William Blake for Thornton's Virgil*. Introduction by Geoffrey Keynes. London, 1938.

William Blake's Designs for Gray's Poems. Reproduced with an Introduction from the unique copy belonging to His Grace the Duke of Hamilton. With an Introduction by H.J.C. Grierson. London, 1922. Facsimile edition, London (Trianon Press), 1972.

Milton, John. *Poems in English*. With illustrations by William Blake. London, 1926. 2 vols.

Illustrations of the Book of Job. Being all the Water-Colour Designs, Pencil Drawings and Engravings Reproduced in Facsimile. Introduction by Laurence Binyon and Geoffrey Keynes. New York, 1935. The engravings have been reproduced in a number of other editions, including ed. Laurence Binyon, London, 1906; ed. Kenneth Patchen, New York, 1947. See also *William Blake's Engravings* (ed. Keynes), below.

Blake's Illustrations to the Divine Comedy. By Albert S. Roe. Princeton, 1953. With an excellent introductory essay and bibliography.

William Blake's Illustrations to the Bible. A Catalogue compiled by Geoffrey Keynes. London (Trianon Press), 1957.

II

A. *Biographies*

Gilchrist, Alexander. *Life of William Blake*. (Completed after the death of Gilchrist by D. G. Rossetti.) London and Cambridge, 1863, 2 vols. Revised and enlarged edn., London, 1880, 2 vols. (References in the text are to the 1880 edition.) The best working edition is that edited by Ruthven Todd for Everyman's Library (London and New York, 1942), with an excellent bibliography.

Wilson, Mona. *The Life of William Blake*. London, 1927. Rev. edn., with additional notes, London, 1948. The standard biography.

B. *Criticism and Interpretation*

Blunt, Anthony. *The Art of William Blake*. New York, 1959.

Erdman, David V. *Blake: Prophet against Empire*. A Poet's Interpretation of the History of His Own Times. Princeton, 1954.

Frye, Northrop. *Fearful Symmetry*. A Study of William Blake. Princeton, 1947. (Beacon paperback, 1962.)

Harper, George Mills. *The Neoplatonism of William Blake*. Chapel Hill, 1961.

Hirst, Désirée. *Hidden Riches: Traditional Symbolism from the Renaissance to Blake*. London, 1964.

Schorer, Mark. *William Blake: The Politics of Vision*. New York, 1946. (Vintage paperback, 1959.)

Todd, Ruthven. "William Blake and the Eighteenth-Century Mythologists." In: *Tracks in the Snow*. Studies in English Science and Art. London, 1946.

Yeats, William Butler. "William Blake and his Illustrations to the Divine Comedy" and "William Blake and the Imagination." In: *Ideas of Good and Evil*. London, 1903. Reprinted in *Essays and Introductions*. London, 1961. The essay, *The Necessity of Symbolism*, in vol. I of the Ellis and Yeats edition of Blake's *Works*, is also by W. B. Yeats.

III

C. *Other Books Referred To*

Aeschylus. *The Tragedies*. Translated by R. Potter. Norwich, 1777.

Agrippa von Nettesheim, Heinrich Cornelius. *Three Books of Occult Philosophy*. Translated by J. F. London, 1651.

Apuleius, Lucius. *The .XI. Bookes of the Golden Asse*. Translated by William Adlington. London, 1566.

Bacon, Francis. *The New Atlantis*. In: *Sylva Sylvarum*, or, A Natural History. Published by William Rawley. London, 1627.

Bacon, Roger. *The Mirror of Alchimy*. Translated by Thomas Creede. London, 1597.

Barrett, Francis. *The Magus, or Celestial Intelligencer*. London, 1801. 2 parts.

Bayley, Harold. *The Lost Language of Symbolism*. London, 1912. 2 vols.

Berkeley, George. *Works*. Edited by A. A. Luce and T. E. Jessop. London, 1948–57. 9 vols.

[Boehme, Jacob.] *The Works of Jacob Behmen*. [Edited by G. Ward and T. Langcake.] London, 1764–81. 4 vols. This is the edition commonly known under the name of William Law. Each work in each volume is separately paginated.

Bryant, Jacob. *A New System, or an Analysis of Ancient Mythology: Wherein an Attempt is made to divest Tradition of Fable, and to Reduce the Truth to its Original Purity*. London, 1774–76. 3 vols.

Burnet, Thomas. *Archaeologiae Philosophicae: sive Doctrina antiqua de rerum originibus libri duo*. London, 1692.

——. *The Theory of the Earth, and of its Proofs*. London, 1690.

Dante Alighieri. *The Divina Commedia*. Translated into English Verse by the Rev. Henry Boyd. London, 1802. 3 vols.

——. *The Inferno*. Translated by H. F. Cary. London, 1805–6. 2 vols.

Davies, Edward. *Celtic Researches, on the Origin, Traditions, and Language of the Ancient Britons*. London, 1804.

——. *The Mythology and Rites of the British Druids*. London, 1809.

Descartes, René. *Principles of Philosophy, and a Voyage to the World of Cartesius*. Written originally in French [by G. Daniel], and now translated into English [by T. Taylor]. London, 1692.

Fludd, Robert. *Mosaicall Philosophy, grounded upon the essential truth or eternal sapience*. Written first in Latin, and afterwards thus rendered into English. London, 1659.

——. *Philosophia Sacra*. Frankfurt, 1626.

Freud, Sigmund. "The Theme of the Three Caskets." Translated by C.J.M. Hubback. In *Complete Psychological Works*, vol. 12. London, 1958.

Geoffrey of Monmouth. *The British History*. Translated by Aaron Thompson. London, 1817.

[Hermes Trismegistus.] *The Divine Pymander of Hermes Mercurius Trismegistus*. Translated from the Arabic by Dr. [John] Everard [1650]. With an introduction by Hargrave Jennings. London, 1884.

Homer. *The Iliad and Odyssey*. Translated into English blank verse by W. Cowper. London, 1791. 2 vols.

——. *The Whole Works of Homer, Prince of Poetts, in his Iliads, and Odysses*. Translated according to the Greek. By George Chapman. London, [1612]. 2 parts.

Johnson, Samuel. *The History of Rasselas, Prince of Abissinia*. Edited by R. W. Chapman. Oxford, 1927.

Jones, Sir William. *Works*. London, 1807. 13 vols.

Jones, Sir William. "On the Gods of Greece, Italy, and India," *Asiatick Researches* (Calcutta), I (1788), 221–75.

Macpherson, James. *An Introduction to the History of Great Britain and Ireland*. 2nd edn., enlarged, London, 1772.

——. *The Works of Ossian*. Translated by James Macpherson. 3rd edn., London, 1765. 2 vols.

Mahony, Capt. "On *Singhala*, or *Ceylon*, and the Doctrines of Bhooddha, from the Books of the *Singhalais*," *Asiatick Researches* (Calcutta), VII (1801), 32–56.

Mallet, Paul Henri. *Northern Antiquities*. Translated [by Bishop Percy]. London, 1770. 2 vols.

Mankowitz, Wolf. *The Portland Vase and the Wedgwood Copies*. London, 1952.

Mead, G.R.S. *Orpheus*. London, 1896.

Morley, Edith J. (ed.). *Blake, Coleridge, Wordsworth, Lamb, etc.* Being Selections from the Remains of Henry Crabb Robinson. Manchester, London and New York, 1922.

Mosheim, Johanna Lorenz von. *An Ecclesiastical History, Antient and Modern*. Translated by A. Maclaine. London, 1765. 2 vols.

Newton, Isaac. *The Mathematical Principles of Natural Philosophy*. Translated by Andrew Motte. London, 1729. 2 vols.

——. *Opticks*. London, 1704. 3rd edn., corrected, London, 1721.

Ovid (Publius Ovidius Naso). *Fasti or the Romans Sacred Calendar*. Translated by W. Massey. London, 1757.

——. *Metamorphoses*. In fifteen books. Translated by the most Eminent Hands [J. Dryden and others]. Edited by Sir Samuel Garth. London, 1717.

Paracelsus (Theophrastus Bombast of Hohenheim). *Archidoxes* [and other works]. Translated by J. H. [? James Howell]. London, 1661. 2 parts.

——. *Aurora and Treasure of the Philosophers*. Translated by J. H. London, 1659.

——. *Nine Books on the Nature of Things*. See Sendivogius.

——. *Of the Chymical Transmutation, Genealogy and Generation of Metals and Minerals*. . . . Translated by R. Turner. London, 1657.

——. *Philosophy Reformed & Improved in four Profound Tractates . . . Discovering the Wonderfull Mysteries of the Creation, by Paracelsus: being his Philosophy to the Athenians*. Translated by R. Turner. London, 1657.

Percy, Thomas. *Reliques of Ancient English Poetry*. London, 1765. 3 vols.

——. See also Mallet.

Plato. See Taylor (5, 6).

Plotinus. See Taylor (1, 8).

Plutarch. *Morals*. Translated from the Greek by Several Hands [M. Morgan, S. Ford, W. Dillingham, T. Hoy, etc.]. 4th edn., London, 1704. 5 vols. (1st edn., 1684–94.) ("Of the Face, appearing within the Orb of the Moon," tr. A. G., *Gent.*, vol. 5, pp. 217–74.)

——. *Treatise of Isis and Osiris*. Translated by Samuel Squire. Cambridge, 1744. 2 parts.

Priestley, Joseph. *A Comparison of the Institutions of Moses with Those of The Hindoos*. Northumberland, Pennsylvania, 1799.

——. *An History of Early Opinions Concerning Jesus Christ*. Birmingham, 1786. 4 vols.

Proclus. See Taylor (3, 7).

Robinson, Henry Crabb. See Morley.

Rousseau, Jean-Jacques. *Eloisa: or, a Series of Original Letters*. Translated [by William Kenrick]. London, 1784. 4 vols.

Sendivogius, Michael. *A New Light of Alchymie; . . . also Nine Books of the Nature of Things, written by Paracelsus . . .* etc. Translated out of the Latin by J[ohn] F[rench]. London, 1650.

Sophocles. *The Tragedies*. Translated by Thomas Francklin. London, 1759. 2 vols.

——. *The Tragedies*. Translated by Robert Potter. London, 1788.

Stuart, James, and Revett, Nicholas. *The Antiquities of Athens, measured and delineated*. London, 1762–1816. 4 vols.

Stukeley, William. *Abury, A Temple of the British Druids*. London, 1743.

——. *Stonehenge, a Temple Restored to the British Druids*. London, 1740.

Stukeley, William. *A Letter . . . to Mr Macpherson on his Publication of Fingal and Temora*. London, 1763.

Swedenborg, Emanuel. *Arcana Coelestia*. Translated by a Society of Gentlemen [actually, John Clowes]. London, 1802–12. 13 vols.

——. *The Doctrine of the New Jerusalem concerning the Lord*. 3rd edn., London, 1791.

——. *The Heavenly Doctrine of the New Jerusalem*. London, 1792.

——. *A Treatise Concerning Heaven and Hell*. [Translated by W. Cookworthy and T. Hartley.] London, 1778.

——. *A Treatise concerning the Last Judgement*. London, 1788.

——. *A Continuation concerning the Last Judgement, and the Spiritual World*. London, 1791.

——. *True Christian Religion; containing the Universal Theology of the New Church*. London, 1781. 2 vols.

——. *The Wisdom of Angels concerning Divine Love and Divine Wisdom*. London, 1788.

——. *The Wisdom of Angels concerning the Divine Providence*. London, 1790.

Taylor, Thomas. [Note: In view of the importance of Taylor as the source of Blake's knowledge of the Platonic philosophy, I have listed all his relevant works published up to and including 1805, the date of

Blake's *Milton*. He continued to publish until 1834, but his later works do not seem to have influenced Blake's thought.] A complete bibliography of Taylor's works is given in *Thomas Taylor the Platonist: Selected Writings*. Ed. Kathleen Raine and George Mills Harper. (Bollingen Series LXXXVIII.) Princeton, 1969.

(1) *Concerning the Beautiful, or a paraphrased translation from the Greek of Plotinus, Ennead I, Book 6*. London, 1787. (Reprinted as *An Essay on the Beautiful*, London, 1792.)

(2) *The Mystical Initiations, or, Hymns of Orpheus. Translated from the . . . Greek, with a Preliminary Dissertation on the Life and Theology of Orpheus*. London, 1787. (2nd edn., *The Hymns of Orpheus*, London, 1792; 3rd edn., *The Mystical Hymns of Orpheus*, London, 1824.)

(3) *The Philosophical and Mathematical Commentaries of Proclus on the First Book of Euclid's Elements . . . to which are added, the History of the Restoration of the Platonic Theology by the Latter Platonists, and a Translation . . . of Proclus' Elements of Theology*. London, 1788–89. 2 vols. (2nd edn., 1792; rev. edn., 1823: see below, no. 18.) ("On the Cave of the Nymphs," vol. 2, pp. 278–307.)

(4) *A Dissertation on the Eleusinian and Bacchic Mysteries*. Amsterdam, [1790]. (Appeared also in *The Pamphleteer*, vol. 8, London, 1816.)

(5) (tr.) *The Phaedrus of Plato*. London, 1792.

(6) (tr.) *The Cratylus, Phaedo, Parmenides and Timaeus of Plato*. London, 1793.

(7) (tr.) *Sallust on the Gods and the World; and the Pythagoric Sentences of Demophilus, translated from the Greek; and Five Hymns by Proclus . . . with a Poetical Version*. London, 1793.

(8) (tr.) *Five Books of Plotinus*. London, 1794.

(9) (tr.) *The Fable of Cupid and Psyche, translated from . . . Apuleius*. London, 1795.

[Vaughan, Thomas.] *Anima Magica Abscondita, or, A Discourse of the Universall Spirit of Nature*. By Eugenius Philalethes. London, 1650.

——. *Anthroposophia Theomagica; or a Discourse of the Nature of Man and his State after Death*. By Eugenius Philalethes. London, 1650.

——. *Aula Lucis, or The House of Light . . .* By S. N., a Modern Speculator. London, 1652.

——. *Coelum Terrae*. See *Magia Adamica*, below.

——. *Euphrates, or The Waters of the East*. By Eugenius Philalethes. London, 1655.

——. *Lumen de Lumine, or, A New Magicall Light*. By Eugenius Philalethes. London, 1651.

———. *Magia Adamica, or, The Antiquitie of Magic. . . .* whereunto is added. . . . *Coelum Terrae.* By Eugenius Philalethes. London, 1650.

———. *The Works of Thomas Vaughan: Eugenius Philalethes.* Edited by A. E. Waite. London, 1919.

Virgil. *Works: containing his Pastorals, Georgics, and Aeneis.* Translated into English Verse by John Dryden. London, 1697.

Warburton, William. *The Divine Legation of Moses.* 4th rev. and enl. edn., London, 1755–65. 5 vols. in 7 parts.

Watts, Isaac. *Divine Songs attempted in Easy Language for the Use of Children.* 9th edn., London, 1728. Another edn., Kidderminister [? 1790].

Wilkins, Sir Charles (tr.). *The Bhagvat-Geeta, or Dialogues of Kreeshna and Arjoon.* London, 1785.

Winckelmann, J. J. *Reflections on the Paintings and Sculptures of the Greeks.* Translated by H. F[üssli]. London, 1765.

Yeats, William Butler. *Autobiographies.* London, 1926; 2nd edn., 1955.

———. *Collected Plays.* London, 1934; 2nd edn., 1952.

———. *Collected Poems.* 2nd edn., London and New York, 1950.

———. (ed.). *The Oxford Book of Modern Verse, 1892–1935.* Oxford, 1936.

———. *A Vision.* London, 1925; 2nd edn., 1937.

1 The sea of time and space: the Arlington Court tempera painting (1821)

2 "All radiant on the raft the Goddess stood": design by Flaxman (1805?) for the *Odyssey*. The theme Blake incorporated into his painting was current in his circle.

3 Frontispiece to *Songs of Innocence* (1789)

4 Beatrice in her car: illustration no. 88 (1826) for Dante's *Paradiso*

5 "The Soul exploring the recesses of the Grave": design for Blair's *Grave* (1808). The cave or grave, following the Platonic philosophers, is this world. The male figure, above, appears to be (like Thel) "listening to the voices of the ground."

6 Nymphs weaving and others carrying urns: detail (right part) of the
Arlington Court picture (1821). Note the olive trees on the promontory
above the Greek porticoed house on left; in top center the nymph pouring
water from an urn and the reclining lovers; top right, winged figures
carrying urns; and main group of weaving nymphs holding shuttles, the
little figure on left woven into the garment, the reclining sleeping figure
sinking into the water, the arm outstretched over a bucket or tub, and the
central ascending figure holding in her hand a full bucket. Also the stone
beam of the "loom" behind the shuttles held by nymphs.

And in the North Gate, in the West of the North, toward Beulah
Cathedrons Looms are builded, & Los's Furnaces in the South
A wondrous golden Building; immense with ornaments sublime
Is bright Cathedrons golden Hall, its Courts Towers & Pinnacles

And one Daughter of Los sat at the fiery Reel & another
Sat at the shining Loom with her Sisters attending round
Terrible their distress & their sorrow cannot be utterd
And another Daughter of Los sat at the Spinning Wheel
Endless their labour, with bitter food, void of sleep,
Tho hungry they labour: they rouze themselves anxious

7 The daughters of Los at the wheel: *Jerusalem* (1804–1820), plate 59, detail

8 The Virgin Mary watched by two angels: illustration (1816?) to Milton's *Paradise Regained*

9 The Virgin Mary with a spinning wheel and distaff encircled by a vine: detail from illustration to the *Divine Comedy* (1827), No. 3 Roe

10

11

10 Woven entrails: design (early 1790's) for Gray's *The Fatal Sisters*

11 Fate severing the thread with shears: detail from Blake's water-color drawing (early 1790's) illustrating Gray's *Ode on the Death of a Favourite Cat*. Compare with Atropos with shears in Arlington Court tempera, and figure with single shear in [17].

12 Sacred cave in a fiery mountain (Mons Argaeus): Bryant's *Mythology*, vol. 1 (1774), plate I

13 Temple of Mithras: Bryant's *Mythology*, vol. 1 (1774), plate V, signed by Basire but possibly by Blake. Note the flames on the altar.

14 The chariot of the sun: detail (upper left corner) of the Arlington Court picture (1821)

15 "Then went Satan forth from the presence of the Lord": engraving for *Job* (1826), plate 5, detail. Compare the drowsy figure of God with the sleeping god in car [1, 14, 82].

16 Eve rising from the sleep of Adam: detail from *Jerusalem* (1804–1820), plate 31

17 "The River of Life": water-color drawing (1805?). Note shear in hand of stooping figure, and radiant figures surrounding sun.

18 Title page designed by Blake for Blair's *Grave* (1808). Compare the "Door of Death" with the "Gates of Birth" [19].

19 "A chapel all of gold": detail from *Vala* MS (1795–1804?), p. 44 Bentley. The symbolic representation of the female genitals as a shrine or chapel may be taken as a representation of Enitharmon's threefold golden gates of birth. Blake is following the tradition which calls the Blessed Virgin the "Domus aurea" (House of gold) in the Litany addressed to her. Cf. the "Door of Death" [18].

20 Title page of *The Book of Thel* (1789). Blake describes fairies as spirits of vegetation, here associated with the pasqueflower of the vegetation-god Adonis.

21 *Infant Joy* from *Songs of Innocence* (1789)

22 Detail of page 21 from Blake's Notebook, with flower drawing illustrating the first lines of Shakespeare's fifteenth sonnet. The theme of the sonnet is growth and decay; Blake has therefore introduced the "fairies" of vegetation.

23 Lovers in a water-lily:
Jerusalem (1804–1820),
detail from plate 28.
Fairies or spirits of
vegetation in a lily or
"lotus of the water."

24 Mourners weeping
over effigies of the dead:
title page of *Songs of
Experience* (1794)

25 "The Conjugal Union of Cupid and Psyche": engraving by Blake for Cumberland's *Thoughts on Outline* (1796). Note the butterfly emblem of the soul.

26 Vala on a sunflower: *Jerusalem* (1804–1820), plate 53, upper half. Note the sun, moon, and stars in her wings.

27 Eve, Adam, and the serpent (1799?). Eve, encircled by the coils of the serpent matter, is represented "near the fall of a river."

28 Marriage of Cupid and Psyche: engraving (from antique medallion) by Bartolozzi for Bryant's *Mythology*, vol. 2 (1774), at p. 393. Eros is a naked figure, Psyche entirely veiled, from head to feet. Note her butterfly wings.

In thunders ends the voice. Then Albions Angel wrathful burnt
Beside the Stone of Night; and like the Eternal Lions howl
In famine & war, replyd. Art thou not Orc, who serpent form'd
Stands at the gate of Enitharmon to devour her children;
Blasphemous Demon, Antichrist, hater of Dignities:
Lover of wild rebellion, and transgresser of Gods Law;
Why dost thou come to Angels eyes in this terrific form?

29 Luvah and Vala asleep with ram, tree, and birds: *America* (1793), plate
7. Tree, birds, and prostrate figure closely resemble similar figures in [35]
and [37].

30 Soul embraced by divine lover: *Jerusalem* (1804–1820), plate 99

31 *The Sick Rose* from *Songs of Experience* (1789–94)

32 The Portland vase: engraving by Blake for Darwin's *Botanic Garden* (1791)

33 The first compartment of the Portland vase

34 The second compartment of the Portland vase

35

37

36

35 The first plate of *The Little Girl Lost* from *Songs of Experience* (1789–94). Note the "luring bird" which, with the "weeping" tree, is also shown in [29].

36 The second plate (upper half) of *The Little Girl Lost* from *Songs of Experience* (1789–94)

37 The third page of *The Little Girl Found* from *Songs of Experience* (1789–94). Compare the reclining figure of Lyca with similar figure of Vala [29], reclining beside not a lion but a ram; and the double trunk with [27].

38 Bromion and Oothoon chained at the mouth of a cave: *Visions of the Daughters of Albion* (1793), frontispiece

39 Oothoon fettered in a wave: *Visions of the Daughters of Albion* (1793), plate 6, detail. Compare fettered foot of Oothoon with fettered feet of Bromion [38].

38

39

41 Ceres with poppies of sleep and corn of resurrection: engraving by Chambars for Bryant's *Mythology*, vol. 2 (1774), plate IX

40 "The Human Harvest": *Milton* (1804–1808), p. 50. The central figure is presumably Ahania "the vegetater happy," who in Blake's mythology corresponds to Ceres.

Whatever is Born of Mortal Birth,
Must be consumed with the Earth
To rise from Generation free;
Then what have I to do with thee?
The Sexes sprung from Shame & Pride
Blowd in the morn; in evening died
But Mercy changd Death into Sleep;
The Sexes rose to work & weep.

Thou Mother of my Mortal part,
With cruelty didst mould my Heart.
And with false self-decieving tears,
Didst bind my Nostrils Eyes & Ears

Didst close my Tongue in senseless clay
And me to Mortal Life betray:
The Death of Jesus set me free,
Then what have I to do with thee?

It is Raised
a Spiritual Body

42 *To Tirzah* (1801) from
Songs of Experience

43 Tharmas turns the "circle of Destiny": *Vala* MS (1795–1804?), p. 82
Bentley. Destiny is ruled by the stars; this is indicated by their depiction
upon the circle held by Tharmas. Compare with Freher's cosmological
diagrams for Law's Boehme [73, 74].

44 Generated soul woven into the filmy woof: *Jerusalem* (1804–1820), plate 37, detail

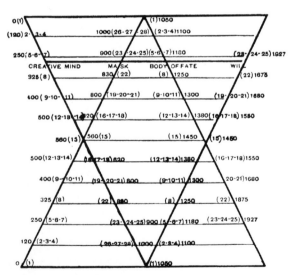

45 Yeats's gyres: diagram from *A Vision* (2nd edn.), p. 266. Headed "The Historical Cones," with this explanation: "The numbers in brackets refer to phases, and the other numbers to dates A.D. The line cutting the cones a little below 250, 900, 1180 and 1927 shows four historical *Faculties* related to the present moment. May 1925."

46 Birth of Orc: *The Marriage of Heaven and Hell* (1790–93?), plate 3, bottom detail

47 Orc fettered by Los and Enitharmon: *America* (1793), plate 2. Compare the figure in "The Mental Traveller" as described on p. 309. The small figure below the roots may be Orc in "deepest hell"; see p. 342, l. 22.

48 Dionysus with his alter ego: Greek vase painting

49 Albion sacrificed by women with knives and a cup ("to catch his shrieks"?): *Jerusalem* (1804–1820), plate 69, detail. The woman on left holds an object which may be the torn-out heart of the victim. Compare [85], where Albion's heart or viscera are being drawn out by women; and [42], "To Tirzah."

50 Jeroboam with withered arm: pen and water-color wash

51 Orc in the fires of energy: *America* (1793), plate 10

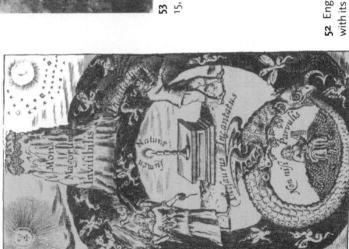

53 Eagle and serpent: *The Marriage of Heaven and Hell* (1790–93?), plate 15, detail. Alchemical emblem of the contraries.

54 Urizen pursued by a cockatrice or basilisk: *America* (1793), plate 4, detail. This basilisk figure may be taken from Vaughan's *Lumen* [52].

52 Engraving in Vaughan's *Lumen de Lumine* (1651). The serpent or basilisk with its tail in its mouth is an emblem of matter often used by the alchemists.

56 Matron Clay: *Thel* (1789), plate 5

55 The worm in her winding sheet: *For Children: The Gates of Paradise* (1793), plate 16. Compare small female figure encircled by basilisk in [52], and the reference to the "fibrous roots," p. 117, l. 2, and [47] (bottom left). Note face of the dead in right foreground.

57 Spirits of heaven and hell: title page of *The Marriage of Heaven and Hell* (1790–93?)

58 Angel and devil: *The Marriage of Heaven and Hell* (1790–93?), plate 4, bottom detail

59 Five giants sunk in the soil: illustration no. 60 (1826) for Dante's *Inferno*. Possibly they represent the five senses.

60 New-born Orc in flames: *Urizen* (1794), plate 20, detail

61 The Tiger. By George Stubbs (1769?)

62 Figures with wreathed torches: detail of Blake's sketch (1810?) for the Last Judgment. On the analogy of Hecate the vegetative principle is represented with three heads.

64 Urizen with tables and book of the law beneath the enrooted tree of nature: title page of *Urizen* (1794).

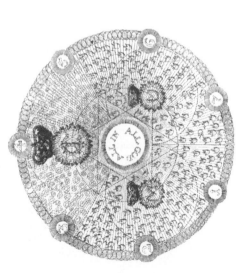

63 Cosmological table by D. A. Freher in Law's Boehme (1764), vol. 2, plate XIII. The seven fountain spirits, and "myriads of flames" within the primal creative fires of the Father. The seals of Solomon may illustrate the *Signatura Rerum*, the stamping with solid form to which Blake refers. Cf. [87].

66 "A Poison Tree" from *Songs of Experience*
(1789–94)

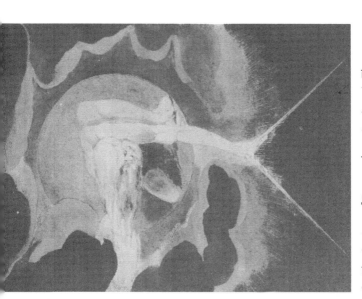

65 The Ancient of Days: color print (1794). The
Creator (of the temporal world) is leaning out of the
sphere of eternity or the soul in order to measure out
in "the void" a universe external to mind or intellect.

67 Raphael conversing with Adam and Eve, with the Tree in the background: water color (1808) illustrating *Paradise Lost*. See also [27, 37].

69 Creation of Adam: tempera color printed monotype (1795). Adam is the natural man or "mortal worm" made of clay.

70 Los (and specter) with hammer, anvil, and furnace: *Jerusalem* (1804–1820), plate 6, detail

68 "I found him beneath a Tree": *For Children: The Gates of Paradise* (1793), plate 8. The female figure draws the child from the ground like a mandrake.

69

70

71 "God blessing the seventh day" (the seven creative spirits): water color (1803?)

72 David delivered out of many waters: water color. The angelic figure above appears surrounded by seven spirits, clearly differentiated according to the traditional qualities.

73 Cosmological table by Freher in Law's Boehme (1764), vol. 2, plate VIII. The stars in the round globe of heaven, raining down influences, the planets each in their sphere. Cf. [43].

74 Same, plate XI. The seven spirits within the zodiac; the serpentine curve illustrates the track by which Jesus entered creation.

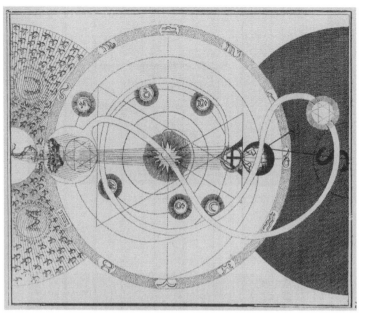

73

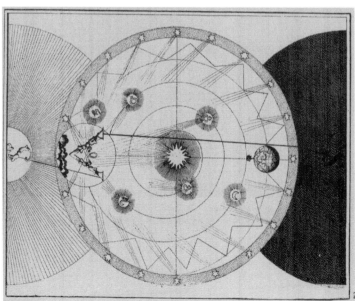

74

75 Four fallen starry ones (the Zoas?): *Jerusalem* (1804–1820), plate 54, bottom detail

76 Newton on the sea floor: color print (1795). Note the white cloth ("the woof of Locke"?) issuing from behind the head of the scientist.

77 *There Is No Natural Religion*
(second series, 1788), p. 9

78 Frontispiece to *For Children: The Gates of Paradise* (1793)

79 "One Law for the Lion & Ox is Oppression":
The Marriage of Heaven and Hell (1790–93?),
plate 24

80 Satan in his original glory: water color. Lucifer's realm is the "starry floor" of nature upon which he walks. He is the demiurge, "prince of the starry wheels" of Destiny. Note the elemental spirits of Nature which surround him.

81 The plow of Jehovah drawn by the horses of Palamabron: *Jerusalem* (1804–1820), plate 33, detail

82 The plow of Jehovah: *Jerusalem* (1804–1820), plate 46, detail. Note Palamabron's horse-hoofed "unicorns" and the "gnomes."

83 The poet pulling down the clay image of the false God with Tables of the Law: *Milton* (after 1804), plate 18

84 Satan with cloven hoof: engraving for *Job* (1826), plate 11, detail. Compare the demiurge creating Adam [69].

83

85 Female powers sacrificing Albion: *Jerusalem* (1804–1820), plate 25 (Coll. Kerrison Preston).

86 Vala drawing out the "veil" of Nature from the body of Albion: *Jerusalem* (1804–1820), plate 85, detail

87 Nature externalized by sacrifice: *Jerusalem* (1804–20), plate 91, detail

84

85

86

87

88 a, b "The Third Table," by Freher, illustrating Law's Boehme (1764). The figure at left represents Man as a microcosm containing within himself both the light and the fire-principles of the divine essence. His feet are in the dark fire-world of the abyss, peopled by monsters; the smoke of generated nature ascends from the fires; sun, moon, and stars are contained within Man's body. Cf. Blake's depiction of Albion [85]. (In these diagrams from Law's Boehme, hinged flaps of paper are lifted to reveal other pictures beneath. "The Third Table" with flaps closed is shown in [88 b].)

89 Job with Elihu: engraving (1826) for *Job*, plate 12

88 b

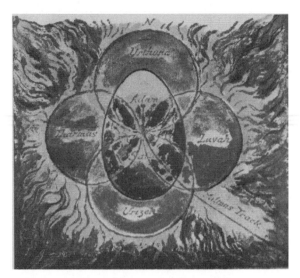

90 Diagram of Mundane Egg and four worlds, surrounded by fire principle of "the Abyss": *Milton* (1804–1808), plate 36, detail. Cf. [74].

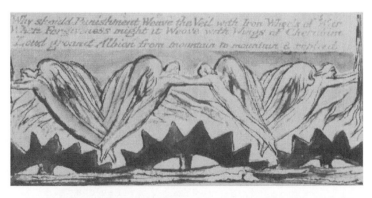

91 Mechanistic causality contrasted with the wings of cherubim: *Jerusalem* (1804–1820), plate 22, detail

Routledge Classics
Get inside a great mind

Marxism and Literary Criticism
Terry Eagleton

'Terry Eagleton is that rare bird among literary critics – a real writer.'
Colin McCabe, The Guardian

A wonderfully clear introduction to the application of Marx's theories to the study of literature. Short and very well-written, it provides a survey of major twentieth-century literary theorists, including Marcuse, Jameson and Lukács. In this ground-breaking work, Eagleton applies viewpoints central to Marxist thought to his analysis. Through this, he is able to show the part that Marxist criticism has to play in defining the crucial link between literature and historical condition.

Hb: 0–415–28583–6   Pb: 0–415–28584–4

The Political Unconscious
Narrative as a socially symbolic act
Fredric Jameson

'Fredric Jameson is generally considered to be one of the foremost contemporary English-language Marxist literary and cultural critics.'
Douglas Kellner

In this ground-breaking and influential study Fredric Jameson explores the complex place and function of literature within culture. At the time Jameson was actually writing the book, in the mid- to late seventies, there was a major reaction against deconstruction and post-structuralism. As one of the most significant literary theorists of the time, Jameson found himself in the unenviable position of wanting to defend his intellectual past yet keep an eye on the future. With this book he carried it off beautifully.

Hb: 0–415–28750–2   Pb: 0–415–28751–0

For these and other classic titles from Routledge, visit
www.routledgeclassics.com

Routledge Classics
Get inside a great mind

Principles of Literary Criticism
I. A. Richards

'To us Richards was infinitely more than a brilliantly new literary critic: he was our guide, our evangelist, who revealed to us, in a succession of astounding lightning flashes, the entire expanse of the Modern World.'
Christopher Isherwood

I. A. Richards was one of the founders of modern literary criticism. *Principles of Literary Criticism* was the text that first established his reputation and pioneered the movement that became known as 'New Criticism'. Highly controversial when first published, this remains a work that no one with a serious interest in literature can afford to ignore.

Pb: 0–415–25402–7

The Wheel of Fire
Interpretations of Shakespearian Tragedy
G. Wilson Knight

'I confess that reading his essays seems to me to have enlarged my understanding of the Shakespearian pattern, which, after all, is quite the main thing.'
T. S. Eliot

Originally published in 1930, this classic of modern Shakespeare criticism proves both enlightening and innovative. Standing head and shoulders over all other Shakespearian interpretations, *The Wheel of Fire* is the masterwork of the brilliant English scholar G. Wilson Knight. Founding a new and influential school of Shakespearian criticism, *The Wheel of Fire* was Knight's first venture in the field – his writing sparkles with insight and wit, and his analyses are key to contemporary understandings of Shakespeare.

Hb: 0–415–25561–9   Pb: 0–415–25395–0

For these and other classic titles from Routledge, visit
www.routledgeclassics.com

Routledge Classics

Get inside a great mind

The Pursuit of Signs
Semiotics, literature, deconstruction
Jonathan Culler

'Twenty years ago, if you wanted to know where literary theory was at, I'd say
"semiotics", and Culler's *The Pursuit of Signs* was the best way to see the
links. Today? Same answer. Overview, criticism, problems and solutions:
Culler offers them all in each chapter, on key topics and questions of the
humanities.'
Mieke Bal, Professor of Theory of Literature, University of Amsterdam

Dancing through semiotics, reader-response criticism, the value of the
apostrophe and much more, Jonathan Culler opens up for every reader
the closed world of literary criticism. To gain a deeper understanding of
the literary movement that has dominated recent Anglo-American literary
criticism, *The Pursuit of Signs* is a must.

Hb: 0–415–25536–8   Pb: 0–415–25382–9

Romantic Image
Frank Kermode

'In this extremely important book of speculative and scholarly criticism Mr
Kermode is setting out to redefine the notion of the Romantic tradition,
especially in relation to English poetry and criticism . . . a rich, packed,
suggestive book.'
Times Literary Supplement

One of our most brilliant and accomplished critics, Frank Kermode here
redefines our conception of the Romantic movement, questioning both
society's harsh perception of the artist as well as poking fun at the artist's
occasionally inflated self-image. Written with characteristic wit and style,
this ingeniously argued and hugely enjoyable book is a classic of its kind.

Hb: 0–415–26186–4   Pb: 0–415–26187–2

For these and other classic titles from Routledge, visit
www.routledgeclassics.com

Routledge Classics
Get inside a great mind

Shakespeare's Bawdy
Eric Partridge

'It reads as freshly today as it did fifty years ago, when it surprised everyone with its originality and daring, and intriguing blend of personal insight and solid detective work. If ever a word-book deserved to be called a classic, it is this.'
David Crystal

Regarded by Anthony Burgess as 'a human lexicographer, like Samuel Johnson', Partridge here combines his detailed knowledge of Shakespeare with his unrivalled knowledge of Elizabethan slang and innuendo to open the window upon a long-avoided aspect of Shakespeare's plays. *Shakespeare's Bawdy* is a work of delight and insight that has an appeal that transcends time and class. Acclaimed by Stanley Wells, editor of *The Oxford Shakespeare*, as 'a classic of Shakespeare scholarship', it takes its place alongside other classics with a well-deserved, if slightly cheeky, impunity.

Hb: 0–415–25553–8   Pb: 0–415–25400–0

What is Literature?
Jean-Paul Sartre

'This is a book that can neither be assimilated nor bypassed. There is probably no better way to encounter it than in this translation, with these notes and this introduction.'
Notes and Queries

Jean-Paul Sartre was one of the most important philosophical and political thinkers of the twentieth century. His writings had a potency that was irresistible to the intellectual scene that swept post-war Europe, and have left a vital inheritance to contemporary thought. In *What is Literature?* Sartre the novelist and Sartre the philosopher combine to address the phenomenon of literature, exploring why we read, and why we write.

Hb: 0–415–25557–0   Pb: 0–415–25404–3

For these and other classic titles from Routledge, visit
www.routledgeclassics.com